THE **27**

**MOST
COMMON
MISTAKES
IN
ADVERTISING**

ALEC BENN

a division of American Management Associations

This book was set in Century Expanded and Spartan Extra Black by Ruttle, Shaw, and Wetherill, Inc.
It was designed by Joan Greenfield

Library of Congress Cataloging in Publication Data

Benn, Alec
   The 27 most common mistakes in advertising.

   Including index.
   1. Advertising. 2. Advertising—Case studies. I. Title.
HF5823.B424   659.1   78-15457
ISBN 0-8144-5478-X
ISBN 0-8144-7554-X

First AMACOM paperback edition 1981.

*Dedicated to two men who took a chance on me
at critical points in my career—*

J. Luttrell Maclin and William A. MacDonough

FOREWORD

Alec Benn is an advertising professional. He has written a professional book about how to get better results from your advertising. His book makes a lot of sense — with no nonsense, no bull, no frills. You won't find one joke in the book. Not one double entendre. Not one autobiographical puff. All you will find is more good common sense about good uncommon advertising than you're likely to find crammed between the covers of any one book.

Mr. Benn has written a book primarily for the advertiser, although advertising agency people can learn much from it. It's a practical guide to getting the most for your advertising dollar. If you have anything to do with spending advertising dollars, this book alone could save you your entire yearly advertising budget.

I don't agree with everything Alec Benn says, but Alec Benn speaks plain, simple, honest truth that can help you get honest and successful advertising. And that's the whole idea.

It seems to me that the 28th biggest mistake you could make in advertising would be not to read Alec Benn's *The 27 Most Common Mistakes in Advertising*.

Hank Seiden
Executive Vice President
Director of Creative Services
Hicks & Greist, Inc.

PREFACE

READ THIS BOOK IF YOU'RE:

an advertising manager, product manager, marketing director, or other executive in a corporation

This book will do more than help you avoid the most common mistakes in commenting on or making decisions about advertising. It will give you a thorough, realistic understanding of what makes advertising effective. This book is designed to help you in two ways. First, it will show you how to make sound judgments about copy, art, type of media, media schedules, research, and billing. Second, it will enable you to deal effectively with people in the advertising agency and within your company. It will help you spot where they are wrong and give you the ammunition you need to convince them of your point of view.

a member of top management of a corporation

This book could save your company hundreds of thousands of dollars by eliminating ineffective advertising and wasteful practices. It will show you how to choose the right kind of agency for your company and how to organize the responsibilities for advertising within your company. It may enable you to increase your sales without increasing your advertising budget. It may help you reduce the cost of recruiting executives and other employees of high caliber.

an account executive or supervisor in an advertising agency, or a media salesman

You'll be able to sell more effectively because you'll know what your clients need. If you're in an agency, you'll become more successful in guiding copywriters, art directors, media analysts, and research directors – and in convincing your boss of the soundness of your recommendations and actions. You'll be able to back up what you say with concrete examples of advertising that has succeeded – and advertising that has failed.

an advertising copywriter

This book gives you a new and complete theory of copywriting that will not only help you move with assurance into new types of advertising copy, but may also help you write better and faster. In addition, it will help you convince your copy supervisor and account executives of the excellence and suitability of the copy you write. It will also prepare you for broader responsibilities.

an art director in an advertising agency

You'll get greater satisfaction out of your job and be able to eliminate much that irritates you. You'll be able to forestall many of the criticisms of copywriters and account executives. You'll create fewer layouts that are rejected, besides preparing yourself for broader responsibilities.

a media analyst in an advertising agency

You'll see the limitations of some of the rules you have been following. You'll be given the fundamentals necessary for the selection of media and preparation of schedules for any product, service, or company for any medium.

an advertising research director

You'll gain a greater understanding of what you are measuring or gathering information for. You'll be given facts that will help you sell the methodology you believe will be most effective.

anyone else who wants to understand what makes advertising
effective or to know what really goes on in the world of
advertising — including instructors, students, and those not now in
advertising who would like to be

Even though this book will be valuable to experienced advertising professionals, it presupposes no knowledge of advertising other than that possessed by an intelligent person living in the United States today.

ABOUT THE CASE HISTORIES AND EXAMPLES

Every case history or example in this book has been judged successful by an objective measure: sales, number of responses, or testing. The results are described so that readers can assess the validity for themselves. A variety of products and services and a broad range of advertising categories are represented, including industrial, image, recruiting, classified, trade — and, especially, direct response and package goods.

In order to create or judge an advertisement correctly, it is necessary to understand how the advertisement fits into the marketing process. A direct response advertisement encompasses in itself more of the marketing process than any other type of advertisement. In its purest form, it begins by attracting the prospect and ends with the sale. Once direct response advertising is understood, it is easier to see what other kinds of advertising should be like in order to be effective.

One well-known copywriter, deservedly enshrined in the Advertising Hall of Fame, said "Every ad I write is a direct response ad. I just change the ending depending upon the situation." He was exaggerating to make a point, but the truth is that much advertising could be improved by following his precept literally.

Package goods advertising differs most importantly from direct response advertising in that the buying decision is delayed. This delay has a significant effect not only on copy but on media selection and on budgets as well.

Since nearly all advertising aims at action — either immediate or delayed — on the part of the reader, viewer, or listener, anyone who has a thorough knowledge of both direct response and package goods advertising is well prepared to deal with or create other kinds of advertising.

In addition, we are on surer ground where results are concerned with direct mail and package goods. The responses from different versions of a direct mail ad can actually be counted. Package goods advertising usually has a direct and measurable effect upon sales. On the other hand, measuring results for other types of advertising, while possible, is less reliable and is a step removed from the usual objective—increasing sales.

Finally, as we shall see, the generally accepted categories of advertising can be misleading. To sum up: the broader the knowledge of advertising, the smaller the likelihood of mistakes and the greater the possibility of effective, even great, advertising.

ACKNOWLEDGMENTS

My thanks to the many advertisers and advertising agencies who contributed case histories and facts about their advertising.

Many thanks also to people at The Magazine Publishers Association, Inc., the American Newspaper Association, *Advertising Age*, and Starch Inra Hooper, Inc.

Special thanks to William A. MacDonough and Caroline M. Benn for reading the manuscript and contributing valuable suggestions.

Alec Benn

CONTENTS

Introduction 1

1. Most Advertising Fails 5

Examples of spectacular advertising failures. Why they're not talked about. How much attention people pay to advertisements. What this book can do for you.

2. Irredeemable Mistakes Sometimes Occur Before the Beginning 9

What happens when the wrong man is put in charge of advertising. Who should be put in charge.

3. Why So Many Advertisers Choose the Wrong Agency 11

Agencies differ in their expertise. Contrasts between requirements for different kinds of advertising.

4. More About Choosing an Agency 18

Relationship between size of agency and size of company's budget. New advertising agencies. Speculative presentations. House agency.

5. Did You See Us on TV? 21

Using TV: the many pluses and the one big minus. Dealer advertising on TV. Budgets. Agencies' competence in media selection.

6. Being Cheap Can Be Expensive 28
Small circulation publications vs. large circulation publications.

7. How Often? 30
When frequency is essential — and when it is not.

8. More About Frequency 32
How the size of the ad affects frequency. Radio and TV. Character of the product or service.

9. How Big? 34
The most economical size for a newspaper advertisement. When ads should be larger, when smaller. Case history of a successful small-budget campaign.

10. Creativity Is All — or Is It? 39
The effect on media decisions of outstanding creativity in copy and art.

11. Beware of Imitations 40
How advertising decisions differ from the usual executive decisions.

12. The Four Commonest Mistakes in Layout and Art 43
How advertising art differs fundamentally from other art. Why nearly all advertising awards are nonsense. Ugly advertisements. How to use art to gain attention and add conviction. Double-page spreads. The special problems of newspaper illustrations. Use of type. How big (or little) should the advertiser's name be?

13. Four Common Mistakes in Copy 55
What draws male readership, what female. What copy should concentrate on. Humor in advertising.

14. How to Get People to Do What You Want with Words and Pictures 59
The only two methods that work. Examples of each method in advertising. How to know when to use which. Why so many advertisers use the wrong method.

15. More About Getting People to Do What You Want 64
Negative motivation. Can the two methods of persuasion be combined?

16. A New and Complete Theory of Copywriting 77

Five sound traditional copy principles. When each is wrong. The six conditions that determine the best ways to write an advertisement. Several kinds of endings. When to be concrete and familiar, when to be abstract and flowery. Several kinds of beginnings. Short vs. long copy. The importance of triviality. The effect of the medium: print, radio, TV, billboard. Correct and incorrect grammar. Young vs. old audiences. High-income audiences. The importance of the nature of the product, service, or company. When positioning is important. What to do when you're not #1. What to do when you *are* #1. How to turn a brand's competitive position into an advantage.

17. Success: If You Don't Measure It, How Do You Know It Exists? 103

Why it's important to have an objective measure of the advertising's effectiveness. The Starch method. Starch scores vs. number of responses. Remembering the ad instead of the product. Recall of sales points. Measuring conviction. Test markets. Focus interviews. Split runs. Awareness-and-attitude surveys. When is a mail survey valid?

18. The Fundamental Mistake Beginners Make with Direct Mail 124

Three common mistakes made by amateurs. How a direct mail letter differs from an ordinary letter. The importance of record-keeping. The one fundamental mistake.

19. Are Advertising Agencies Overpaid? 128

The 15 percent system. When and how agencies make big profits. Where the money goes. The handicap of the small budget and how to overcome it.

20. Six Mistakes Made by Critics of Advertising 132

1. "Advertising makes people buy things they don't need." 2. "Advertising makes products cost more." 3. "Good restaurants don't advertise." 4. "Advertising is a bunch of lies." 5. "Advertising insults the intelligence." 6. "I never buy anything because of the advertising."

21. The 27 Most Common Mistakes in Advertising and How to Avoid Them: A Review 138

With recommendations for appropriate preventive action.

22. Why Some Advertising Succeeds 143

The importance of the relationship between the agency and the advertiser. The responsibilities of each and how to make them work. Twenty key questions the advertising agency should ask a new client or prospect. Ten key questions the advertiser should ask about the agency's recommendations. Seven questions to ask when choosing an advertising agency.

Glossary of Commonly Used Advertising Terms 148

Index 153

CASE HISTORIES

How the Chicago office of *Lanier* sold more dictating equipment than ever before. 15

How *Moody's* sold books at $12 each through space advertising 17

How *ITT* cut in half the number of people who confuse it with AT&T 25

How *Federal Express* became first in awareness among freight forwarders in three years 27

How *Tylenol* captured 10 percent of the $440 million analgesic market 37

How *Parker Pen* doubled sales in four years, reaching over $117 million 49

How *Volkswagen* became the largest-selling imported car in the United States 51

How *Alexander's, Inc.* attracted hundreds of additional shoppers with a single advertisement 53

How *Bodine* successfully promoted sales of capital equipment in a recession year 66

How annual sales of *Virginia Slims* climbed from zero to nearly eight million cigarettes in seven years 69

How the *Marine Corps* successfully competed for recruits with
a much smaller budget than the other services 71

How a major investment firm successfully recruited
brokers of high caliber. 72

How a telephone company reduced costs by over $5 million with
an advertising expenditure of less than $500,000 73

Which help-wanted ad pulled better in each case? 75

How *L'eggs* became the best-selling brand of hosiery in the
United States 92

How *Mitchum* doubled its share of the deodorant market
in less than two years 96

How *Manufacturers Bank* in L.A. used positioning to
increase new accounts by 51 percent in the first year,
61 percent the second 98

How *Diaperene Baby Wash Cloths* became the
fastest-growing brand in its category 99

How *Loctite* spectacularly increased sales of its
pipe sealant in three months 101

Which *General Electric* ad attracted more readers? 114

Which *Gaines-Burger* ad attracted more readers? 118

Elmer's Glue: Which television commercial was
more memorable? 121

How *The Bowery Savings Bank* sold $8 million worth of life
insurance with an advertising expenditure of under $100,000 136

To err is human.
To continue to make the same mistake — stupid!

INTRODUCTION: ON THE NATURE AND VALUE OF ADVERTISING EXPERIENCE

Talented, charming, well-educated people can make more money at an earlier age in an advertising agency than in most other lines of endeavor. And if they develop the ability to attract clients to them personally, they can set up their own agencies and possibly become modestly rich.

For advertising executives in corporations, the monetary rewards are usually less, but experience in advertising can be an important step toward future advancement. In corporations heavily dependent on advertising for sales, such as Procter & Gamble, General Mills, and CPC Corporation, advertising experience is a must for anyone aiming at a top-line position.

But even in a corporation where advertising is less obviously vital, experience in advertising can be advantageous to the ambitious executive. The advertising executive is highly visible to top management. Chief executives usually like to concern themselves with their corporation's advertising. They should, as one of a chief executive's prime responsibilities is the relationship between his corporation and the outside world.

What is more, an advertising executive often has greater opportunities for constructive action than most other executives. Success in many executive positions in large corporations consists largely in avoiding mistakes, and in following a routine that has been established by a predecessor. A new advertising director, however, cannot continue indefinitely to place the same advertising his predecessor did. Sooner or later a new campaign is necessary. Finally, an advertising director who gets a superior campaign out of the advertising agency is likely to get more credit with top management than the agency does. And rightfully so. The responsibility is his. The decision is his. And the career on the line is his.

As valuable as the career rewards can be, the psychological rewards of advertising experience, for people in both the agency and the advertising corporation, can be even greater for the right kind of person.

In an affluent society, the greatest enemy of the educated, energetic, thinking person is not taxes, people on welfare who should be working, politicians, multinational corporations, unions, the Soviet Union, the super-rich, or the radical left, but simply boredom. Advertising is seldom boring. It's always changing. Magazines come and go. Stations revise their programming. Even new types of media are created (in New York, for example, bus-stop shelters and signs atop taxicabs). Some established media become less efficient, some more so. Rates go up, rates go down (hardly ever). TV availabilities become tight – or easy. Advertising budgets are reduced or increased, sometimes requiring an entire rethinking of the advertising strategy, or at least a look at whether rethinking is necessary.

More important, boredom is eliminated because new ideas are essential to advertising. For some, the challenge is to develop new ideas, for others the challenge is evaluation. Besides intelligence, both the creating and the judging require courage. Nobody knows enough about what people respond to and about advertising techniques to be absolutely sure that an advertising campaign will be successful.

The advertising executive must make his judgment on the basis of incomplete knowledge and experience, yet also convince others that his decisions are correct. That's what makes advertising exciting and nerve-racking, depending on the temperament of the executive.

It also means that the sensible advertising executive continually strives to learn more about those advertising techniques that have succeeded in the past and those that have failed. And to increase his or her understanding of what human beings are really like. The more that is known, the greater the odds of being right. A man or woman who is continually searching for knowledge by observing, reading, and experimenting is seldom bored.

The variety of skills required in advertising offer opportunities to specialists and to generalists. People good with words can become copywriters; those with pictures, art directors; those with numbers, media analysts; those with people, account executives or media salesmen. The advertising director of a corporation, however, faces all these challenges. Some of the judgments he must make require logic, others esthetic sensitivity; some are based on statistics, some on the reliability of the source.

The challenges of advertising are appealing because they deal with the real world in an important way: Advertising is essential to the American business system. It shows people how much better life can be and it establishes standards and goals. It causes people to need more money and therefore to strive harder to get it. It stimulates the economy not only with direct sales but also by giving people reasons to work — and to work harder.

Experience in advertising can better equip an executive to deal with big decisions in other areas. All knowledge — not just knowledge of advertising — is incomplete and uncertain. It's just more so in advertising. This means that when the executive with advertising experience is faced with a big decision that requires courage, one where all the facts cannot be known, he will at the minimum be more confident in acting and at best be more likely to be right. He's made decisions like this many times before. He's had on-the-job training.

Many people, however, should avoid going into advertising either as a life-time career or even as a means of advancement. The personality that makes a good military officer, for example, is likely to be wrong for advertising. While many graduates of West Point and Annapolis have gone on to successful careers in business, I know of none who have been successful in advertising. What counts most in the military, and in most big businesses, is doing what is correct according to the judgment of some higher authority. An executive usually has a boss who knows more than he does about the job. Much of the executive's work consists in carrying out the boss's orders with little question. Advertising people, on the other hand, must continually convince superiors who know less than they do of what should be done. To take one upward line of persuasion: the copywriter must convince the copy supervisor that the copy is right, the copy supervisor convince the account executive, the account executive convince the advertising director, and the advertising director convince top management. The initiative comes from below and moves against the chain of authority.

Anyone who believes "You can't fight City Hall" doesn't belong in advertising.

Advertising is not for people who can't find ways to deal with its frustrations. No one feels courageous all the time. The equanimity of the most stalwart executive can be battered into bewilderment by a sufficient number of successive irreconcilable demands.

One executive was often unable to sleep because of conflicts between the kind of advertising he thought was best and the kind his bosses insisted on. He found his solution in "mental health" days. Instead of quitting a job he liked in many respects, or being stubborn, or having three martinis for lunch, or passively acquiescing, he would simply tell himself when sleep eluded, "I'm not going to work tomorrow." It was a perfect soporific. He spent the day loafing, reading, or going to a museum or the movies. Sometimes he broke his nighttime promise to himself and went to work; all he'd needed was a good night's sleep. In any event, he found a way to rebuild his ability to politely, but forcefully and effectively, persuade those in authority. He took perhaps three "mental health" days a year—far fewer than others take for psychosomatic illnesses.

Because so much advertising consists in telling those with power what they ought to do, there are many charming people in advertising. The charming people may sometimes be fraudulent, but at least they *are* charming. There are many talented people in advertising. Some are the opposite of charming, but at least their talent is admirable. And almost anybody who lasts any time at all in advertising is intelligent, alert, and open to new ideas.

Perhaps the greatest rewards in advertising come from dealing with these many charming, talented, intelligent people. They're amusing, stimulating, and edifying. Their combined abilities and characters make it possible to accomplish much in comparatively little time. While each may be an individual star, all are necessary to each other, forcing a team spirit upon even the most individualistic. Together, solutions are arrived at that none could achieve alone. Together, because an advertising campaign may affect the lives of so many people, they can make the world a little different than it was before, generally better, even though materialistically.

To be in advertising is to be more fully alive.

MOST ADVERTISING FAILS

There is a great conspiracy participated in by advertising agencies, radio and television stations and networks, advertising consultants, newspapers, magazines, and others to mislead corporate managements about the effectiveness of advertising. Those who control the purse strings are not told about campaigns costing millions that fail to make any difference in company sales. There was, for example, little publicity about the results of some very entertaining commercials placed by Alka-Seltzer in the early 1970s. Only a few attentive professionals knew Alka-Seltzer did not increase its share of the market.

Advertising men don't talk much about advertisements that damage a company. Did you know that one high-priced consultant has the dubious distinction of creating an advertisement so counterproductive that the president of the company was fired because of it? This advertising genius — and he is a genius of sorts — went on to repeat the performance. He created a campaign for another company with just as negative an effect, and another president was fired! Yet this advertising consultant, when last heard of, was still collecting big fees.

While libel laws make naming this man dangerous, it is not fear of being sued that restrains advertising professionals from telling corporate managements facts they should know.

It is money and human nature.

Corporate managements would spend less on advertising if they knew the true odds against successful advertising.

The conspiracy could not succeed, however, without the willing co-operation of the corporate managers. Many chief executives get big ego boosts out of their company's advertising. They want to believe making advertising decisions is easy, so they act as if it is. They enjoy the feeling and rewards of creativity without the agony and sweat of creating.

One advertising agency—which has many imitators—has made a big success by creating flamboyant, often entertaining, advertisements that chief executives love but that often fail to do their companies any good. This agency had the gall to run a double-page magazine advertisement that included advertisements it had created for companies that were no longer in business. Now, a company may fail for a reason other than its advertising, but in any other field—say, the law—wouldn't revealing failures be a deterrent to obtaining new clients? Yet this agency's advertisements directly resulted in new business. Why? Because many of those who choose advertising agencies and make decisions about advertising don't know how to judge whether or not an advertisement will be effective (they are inclined to think that what they like will be effective)—and, what's worse, they don't want to know any better.

Throughout the advertising profession and in many corporations there are honest, intelligent, competent men and women who don't want to be part of the conspiracy. There are advertising agency people who educate their clients. There are advertising consultants who create effective advertising. There are media salespeople whose recommendations have made the difference between a campaign's success or lack of success. There are advertising managers who know their business. And there are corporate chief executives who are either advertising experts themselves or who listen to those with advertising competence.

But these men and women are few. And they are unevenly dispersed throughout the business world. Some companies have large numbers of competent advertising people—one package goods advertiser, for example, is known to be so capable that it is a mark of distinction to be chosen as one of its advertising agencies.

At the other end of the spectrum are the many companies that advertise, yet have no one in their company capable of making sound advertising decisions—and who don't measure the effectiveness of their advertising so they don't know how bad it is.

If you doubt that most advertising fails, make this test. Pick up yesterday's newspaper. Look through it carefully, page by page, examining every advertisement. Note how many of the advertisements that were meant to influence you had no effect upon you. Not only did you not read them – you didn't even notice them.

You can make the same test with any magazine you've already read. Your experience will corroborate a test conducted by the American Association of Advertising Agencies in 1965. They investigated the number of advertisements people pay at least some attention to during the course of a day. They came up with a figure of 76. Note that the number of advertisements people were exposed to is much higher – 76 is simply the number they paid some attention to. With this kind of competition for people's minds, it is impossible for any but comparatively few advertisements to be effective.

Advertising research shows that few people read all the copy in an advertisement. In fact, the most prevalent research method does not measure how many people read an ad completely, because the figures would be so small as to be meaningless. The most rigorous measurement is "read most" – that is, the percentage of readers who read most of the words in the advertisement.

How many advertisers realize when they approve an advertisement that only a small percentage of the readers of any publication in which it appears will finish reading it? And that only a percentage of that percentage will be favorably influenced?

Despite this, advertising performs a vital and important business function. It is difficult to see how our present high standard of living could have been achieved without mass production to make products cheap, without installment payments to make buying possible, and without advertising to raise people's concept of how much better life can be.

Many people may find this book helpful whether they know much or little about advertising, whether they now occupy – or aim to occupy – sales, creative, or administrative positions. But it can make the greatest difference in advertising if it is read and acted upon by decision makers. This is a book that accurately describes the world of advertising, exposes the forces that make successful advertising rare, and establishes methods for sound decision making – in short, this book can make it less likely that an advertiser will waste his advertising dollars and more likely that his advertising will efficiently achieve its objective. If widely read, it can raise the effectiveness of advertising generally. It can help a corporate executive to be truly respected by his advertising agency and by advertising professionals. It can help all advertising professionals – in agencies and out – who don't want to be part of the conspiracy, to be proud of what they do.

2

IRREDEEMABLE MISTAKES
SOMETIMES OCCUR BEFORE
THE BEGINNING

A chief executive once put his firm's personnel director in charge of advertising. It was not as ridiculous a selection as might appear on the surface. The personnel director was the company's most competent executive. He had his department so well organized he could assume additional duties. And he was a devoted, loyal employee.

The personnel director, after what he considered objective study, launched an advertising program designed to improve the morale of the company's employees. Not an unworthy objective. However, the company was starving for sales at the time and urgently needed advertising that would give salesmen leads.

The moral is not that the sales manager should be in charge of advertising. It is that the responsibilities of the person in charge of advertising should closely coincide with the purpose of the advertising.

If the objective is recruiting, the advertising should be controlled by an executive whose promotion in the company depends upon the success of the recruitment program. If the company sells several products, with the selling effort of each under separate product managers, there should be separate advertising budgets for each product. If the primary objective of the advertising is to improve the company's image, the chief executive should control the advertising.

When the person in charge of advertising does not directly benefit from the success of the advertising, the following often occurs:

The advertising agency is selected on the basis of personal friendship or favors received and anticipated rather than on the advertising agency's merits. (People who have power tend to use that power to further their own ends. And control of a company's advertising is a great deal of power.)

The advertising agency is not given proper direction. (The person in charge of advertising doesn't know precisely which direction to point in. Or he gives the advertising a direction which pleases him esthetically. Or he uses his control of the advertising to scratch the back of another executive as part of the company's internal politics.)

The work that the agency does and the bills it renders are not sufficiently checked by the client. (The person in charge of the advertising doesn't care.)

Note the phrase "person in charge of advertising" rather than "advertising manager" or "advertising director." The holder of the title may or may not have the power to make the key decisions. Often it is the advertising director's boss, usually not himself an advertising professional, who holds the power and makes the big mistakes.

It is the chief executive officer, however, who is responsible for making or avoiding **Common Mistake #1: Putting in charge of advertising a person whose responsibilities do not coincide with the purpose of the advertising.**

When in doubt, the chief executive officer should control the advertising himself.

3

WHY SO MANY
ADVERTISERS CHOOSE
THE WRONG AGENCY

For a non-reponsible person, or a committee, selecting an advertising agency can be a lot of fun. A number of agencies are asked to make speculative presentations. The group sits around like judges while the agency people perform often amusingly, almost always with brilliance. For the committee, it's an escape from their usual routine. It beats working, but does it do the company any good?

For the person to whom the advertising results are critical, choosing an advertising agency can be agony.

He usually begins by deciding whether to ask for speculative presentations – that is, suggested advertisements specially prepared for his company – or whether to judge agencies on their past performances. Each has its pitfalls and advantages. Whichever method he chooses, he must try to look beyond each dazzling presentation for each agency's real competence.

Often none of the agencies he is judging is right for his company, but he doesn't know that the right kind of agency exists because he has already made Common Mistake #2.

Common Mistake #2 arises from a widespread misunderstanding of the different kinds of agencies and the different types of advertising.

Television viewers are most conscious of package goods advertising – advertising for soap, deodorants, razor blades, candy, cigars, bread – products that are sold in packages in drug stores and super-

11

markets. We're all conscious of this kind of advertising because there is so much of it. And because to be effective—this is the key—it must be *memorable*.

Think of what a package goods commercial must do. Viewers see the commercial usually unwillingly. It is thrust upon them. They want to see the program. Yawning viewers must not only be made to want the product, but also to remember the brand name the next day or so when they are in the store—even though there is little or no difference between the brand being advertised and competitive brands.

Many package goods commercials therefore utilize a startling mnemonic device—a white knight, a dove, a nearly naked man, a personality, an amusing incident—to differentiate the brand and to cause viewers to remember the brand name. Often these commercials are true works of art. Many are widely admired as commercials, independent of the products they feature, and rightly so.

The mistake made by many chief executive officers, and by others in charge of advertising, is this: They want their advertising to be as widely admired and remembered as the best package goods television commercials—even though they are not in the package goods business and are not using television.

Other kinds of advertising need not be as memorable as package goods advertising, and in fact at times should not be.

Often it is better to cause the reader or viewer to admire the product or service or company independently of the commercial. If a viewer says, "Wasn't that a great commercial!" isn't he implying that the commercial is at least a partial lie, that it makes the product appear to be better than it really is? Isn't the inference likely to be drawn, inaccurately perhaps, that the product itself is not very good? (Some companies don't advertise precisely because they feel advertising cheapens their product, their service, or their company.)

A greater achievement for a commercial or advertisement may be to cause people to buy the product but say, "I'm never influenced by advertising."

What does all this have to do with choosing an advertising agency?

Agencies differ in their expertise. Some are great at package goods advertising. Some are great at direct response advertising. Some are good at corporate advertising, some at industrial advertising, some at retail advertising, some at trade advertising, some at classified advertising. Some are better at television than others. Some are better at print (that is, in newspapers and magazines).

Some agencies are expert in specific industries such as ethical drugs, finance, or books.

Nearly every agency believes it can create and guide advertising other than the type at which its past successes prove it is best. The reason is this: Most agencies honestly don't realize that the principles and methods they have developed don't apply to other types of advertising.

But there are exceptions.

One great advertising agency got its start in brand name retail advertising, particularly in magazine ads for men's clothing. In this kind of advertising taste is most important. The products must appear to be beautiful. A certain aura must be created. Memorability, while desirable, need not be on the package goods level.

It took the charming genius who founded this agency many years to catch on to the fundamentals of package goods advertising on television. He did so by hiring men with proven successes in package goods, letting them do their thing, watching what they did, and measuring the results.

The requirements for effective mail order advertising—or to use the more inclusive term, direct response advertising—differ radically from those for any other kind of advertising. Out of the 6,000 or so advertising agencies, only a few know how to create effective direct response advertising. Yet the basic principles have been well established ever since a pioneer back in the 1920s counted the coupons his clients received from different types of direct response advertisements, drew solid conclusions based on facts, and published those conclusions.

Here are the basic characteristics of a typical successful direct response advertisement:

First, the headline contains a strong, emotion-arousing benefit for the reader ("Be Slimmer—Fast"), selecting out of the many readers of the publication those most likely to mail the coupon.

Second, the layout attracts the reader's attention and makes it easy for him to read all the copy.

Third, the copy so increases the desire of the reader for what is being offered that he or she goes to all the bother of tearing out the coupon, filling it out, finding an envelope, addressing it, finding a stamp, and mailing the envelope. (See the Moody's ad at the end of this chapter.)

Note that the advertisement need not be tasteful. Many successful direct response ads are ugly. A direct response advertisement need not be memorable, either. If it does not make readers act immediately, it is a failure. (That's why nearly every successful direct response advertisement ends with the injunction, "Act now!" or some other urge to immediate action.)

As you can see, the principles governing successful package goods advertising differ from those governing successful retail advertising, which are in turn different from the principles governing direct response advertising — to take just three of the many varieties of advertising. What's more, most advertising agency professionals don't understand these differences because they haven't had the necessary experience.

If most advertising professionals do not understand that different marketing methods require fundamentally different kinds of advertising, is it any wonder that intelligent nonprofessionals are similarly ignorant?

Because package goods commercials are so spectacularly memorable, the advertising agencies a company selects for consideration are often those that have created the tricky, pleasing commercials that are right for package goods — even though the company may not be in the package goods business and this kind of advertising may be wrong for it.

This is one reason certain companies continually switch from one advertising agency to another. They anticipate each time that they are getting what is currently the most creative agency. What they don't realize is that the agency that may be most admired for its creativity may be right for other companies but wrong for them.

Common Mistake #2: Choosing an advertising agency with the wrong expertise.

It can be avoided — if the purpose of the advertising is to increase sales — by considering only agencies that have increased the sales of products or services that are marketed the same way your company's product or service is marketed. And by using similar logic in choosing an advertising agency for other purposes such as recruiting and investor relations.

If the person responsible for the advertising avoids Common Mistake #2, choosing an agency will be no agony. By inviting only those with appropriate expertise, he makes sure that every agency he sees is likely to be able to create excellent advertising for his firm.

CASE HISTORIES

Below and on the following pages are two case histories that illustrate a number of principles, including the difference between advertising that aims at memorability and advertising that aims at direct response. The agency that created the first needed a thorough knowledge of retail marketing. The agency that created the second needed a thorough knowledge of investing.

LANIER RADIO COMMERCIAL

ANNCR: Stiller and Meara for Lanier Dictating Equipment.

MEARA: I have your secretarial application right here, Mr. Piltdown.

STILLER: Call me Craig.

MEARA: Well, sit down, Craig.

STILLER: I am sitting.

MEARA: Oh (laughter), of course you are . . . my you're huge!

STILLER: I played fullback for the Pennsylvania Anthrocites.

MEARA: How did you get into secretarial work?

STILLER: Well, I was a receptionist. Then one of the girls got pregnant so they just moved me up.

MEARA: Uh, huh.

STILLER: It's not easy being a secretary. I was the only one around that could handle those old-fashioned belted dictating machines. Boy are they hard to load. You see, that's my specialty.

MEARA: You won't be needing that, Craig. We use Lanier cassettes. You've heard of Lanier cassettes?

STILLER: He played with the Texas Cowboys.

MEARA: (Laughter) No. Lanier makes cassette dictating equipment. Cassettes are easier to load and they sound better.

STILLER: No belts. Then you don't need me.

MEARA: Oh yes. I need you. I need you, Craig.

STILLER: Hey lady. . . .

MEARA: Hmmmmmmmmm.

STILLER: You blew in my ear.

MEARA: It's lonely at the top.

STILLER: I'm not that kind of a guy.

MEARA: You'll learn (laughter).

ANNCR: Put standard cassette speed and efficiency in your dictation. Give Lanier a hearing. We're in the Yellow Pages under dictating machines.

The Lanier commercial was aimed at two audiences. One consisted of executives, lawyers, doctors, and others who might go into a store to buy dictating equipment. The purpose of the commercial in relation to this audience was to cause them to remember the name Lanier and be receptive to this brand. The other audience consisted of dealers. They were to be influenced to stock Lanier dictating equipment. It was important, therefore, that the dealers admire the advertising and remember it when the Lanier representative called on them. Note that no audience needed to be convinced, or influenced to take action. In the Chicago market, more than half a million dollars was spent on the campaign, which included similar television commercials and print ads as well. The commercials were bunched into flights — that is, were run at high frequency for short periods — in order to pound the name into the listeners' minds. Surveys were made of executives, lawyers, and doctors before the campaign was begun, and again afterward. Awareness of the brand name Lanier increased from 11 percent of the audience to 32 percent. Preference for the Lanier brand increased from 6 percent to 27 percent. The percentage of people who could recall any Lanier advertising jumped from 3 percent to 55 percent. And the Chicago office of Lanier posted its highest dollar sales volume ever. The advertising agency was Marsteller.

A DOLLAR-PULLING PRINT AD

Every time the advertisement on the opposite page appeared in such publications as *Barron's, Forbes, Fortune, U.S. News & World Report, Financial World, Signature,* and leading financial newspapers, it pulled more dollars than the advertisement cost. And since the buyer needed to buy additional handbooks (one every three months) in order to keep up to date, the Benn & MacDonough, Inc. ad was highly profitable for Moody's. The size was a full page in magazines, a quarter-page in newspapers. Previously, smaller advertisements with shorter copy had been tried but were unsuccessful. Note that it was not necessary for the reader to remember the name Moody's or to admire the advertising. This advertisement was rotated with other similar ads for several years in the late 1960s. Insertions were spaced out, with more intensive frequency possible in some publications than in others. In *Barron's,* for example, advertisements could run as often as every three weeks, but in *U.S. News & World Report,* advertisements could be placed only every six months.

4

MORE ABOUT
CHOOSING AN AGENCY

Question: What about the relationship between the size of the company's advertising budget and the size of the agency it should choose?

Answer: The most important criterion is that the agency be experienced in creating advertising that has proved effective in similar marketing situations. Other considerations are subsidiary, are simply good business common sense. For example, in choosing any supplier a company should check on the work the supplier has done for others. Has the advertising the agency has done for its clients actually increased sales, or improved company images, or brought in suitable recruits? This can be found out by asking the clients. If the advertising has helped them, they will be enthusiastic about the agency. Most clients who have been truly helped by their advertising agencies are grateful. What the agency has done for their business far exceeds the cost to the company. They will be glad to recommend the agency if it has done resultful work for them.

As for the relationship between the size of the company's budget and the size of the agency, practically everything that has been written and said on this topic is nonsense. A company is often advised to make sure that its budget is not near the agency's minimum, that it is in fact well above the agency's average, so that the company will get a great deal of attention. The fact is that for every company that benefits because its budget is above the agency's average, there is a company with a smaller-than-average budget that benefits from extra services and higher caliber advertising personnel.

In short, the relationship between the advertiser's budget and the average-size account in the agency is immaterial.

Question: You state that the agency should have experience in marketing similar products. Does this mean you rule out new advertising agencies, and that agencies should not expand into other types of advertising?

Answer: It is usually safer to choose an agency with appropriate experience. And there are so many capable agencies that a new agency is usually not worth the additional risk. New agencies are often founded by men and women who have made reputations creating spectacular package goods TV commercials. They often get their accounts from non-package-goods clients who choose them for the wrong reasons.

If there is a good reason to choose a new agency or an agency with no successful experience in creating ads for similarly marketed products, the company should at least make sure that the people working on the account have had successful experience of this kind at other advertising agencies.

Question: What about speculative presentations? Should a company ask agencies it is considering to make speculative presentations?

Answer: There is only one valid reason for not asking for speculative presentations, and it is a big one. For competitive reasons, it may not be wise for a company to tell a number of agencies a great deal about its business, because the losing agencies will be put in an excellent position to create advertising for competitors. Yet an agency that is not fully informed about the company and its products or services will find it difficult to create effective advertising. Superficial knowledge may result in superficial advertising. It may look good, but it may not achieve results.

Anyhow, speculative presentations are not necessary if only those agencies are selected for consideration that have proved their competence in creating advertising for similarly marketed products and services.

19

The sensible approach is to select an agency with the clear understanding that the choice is tentative. Feed the agency all the information it needs. Then judge its performance.

Question: What do we need an advertising agency for, anyhow? Why don't we create and place our own advertising?

Answer: It costs the advertiser no more to place advertising through an agency than to place it directly. The agency receives 15 percent of the space or time billings from the publication, network, station, or other medium in which the ad or commercial appears. The copy, media analysis, and order placing done by the agency are, in effect, free to the advertiser.

But costs are not the only consideration. Even if these services were not free, it would be advantageous for the advertiser to use an agency. First, most companies wouldn't pay the high salaries top-notch copywriters and art directors merit. To do so would put the corporation's salary scales out of balance. Second, copywriters and art directors need to work on a variety of advertising to round their skills. Third, it is costly for the company to accumulate the experience with various types of media that an agency gathers automatically. Fourth—and most important—the agency is in a position to be objective. It can see the company and its products from the consumer's viewpoint more easily than employees of the company can.

Question: Is that all this book is going to say about choosing an agency?

Answer: For the moment, yes. The final chapter includes other tools for choosing an agency that can best be utilized after you have read the intervening chapters. That's why they're there—at the end. Practically everything in this book will help in choosing an agency. The more an executive knows about advertising, the better the choice he or she is likely to make. This book is designed not only to give executives a proper understanding of the fundamentals of advertising but also to eliminate many misunderstandings. The worst damage is done by those who are sure of "facts" that simply are not facts at all. Many of these misconceptions concern media, partly because of self-interest, wishful-thinking, and rationalizations, and partly because the effect of different objectives on this decision is not properly understood.

5

DID YOU SEE US ON TV?

The glamour of television seduces some advertisers into costly splurges.

Television is far and away the most effective advertising medium. Advertising can be thought of as a substitute for a personal call by a salesman. Most types of advertising fall far short. Radio supplies only the voice. Print supplies a still picture plus words, but without the emotional tones of personal delivery. Television combines emotionally inflected words with pictures that move.

Television is really another form of communication, rather than another form of advertising. It causes the viewer to feel that he has been carried to the location pictured on the screen. Entertainers on TV are wont to say, "Thanks for letting us come into your living room." They've got it wrong. Emotionally, viewers feel that they have been magically transported to where the entertainer is.

The trouble with TV is that it costs so much. Costs of advertising on television vary with the time of day or night, whether a show is sponsored or spots are bought, and the bargaining power of the advertiser.

A one-minute commercial on the average network sports program, for example, might cost from $30,000 to more than $75,000 — let's say $50,000. Two million dollars, as simple arithmetic shows (2,000,000 ÷ 50,000), will buy 40 minutes per year. That's less than one minute per week. If 30-second commercials are used, 80 commercials could be placed during the year.

When you consider how many commercials there are on television, when you remember that viewers want to see the program and not the commercials, and when you think how fast 30 seconds go by, doesn't common sense indicate that a minimum of $2 million is a sensible rule of thumb for national exposure if viewers are to remember the brand name of the product and be motivated to buy that brand?

A lower minimum is possible if the marketing system does not make it necessary for the buyer to ask for the product by brand name or otherwise select it. Television can be effectively used only to influence the *dealer* to recommend the product to his customers, and to cause the buyer to recognize the brand name when the dealer volunteers it. Dealers are highly conscious of the advertising of the products they sell. Other things being equal, they will recommend an advertised brand rather than one that is not. They know that customer acceptance will be higher and the sale will be easier.

For a national market, $500,000 might be enough for a campaign primarily designed to influence dealers. Less than that is likely to result in the commercials and the products or services they feature being as well remembered by viewers as the third violinist in a symphony orchestra.

Yet many advertisers with small budgets who must directly motivate buyers want to be on television. This kind of client tempts its advertising agency. Most agencies would rather place television than any other kind of advertising. There's usually more profit for the agency. It takes less creative time to write and produce a single commercial than to write and design a number of print advertisements. And the agency's creative people would rather see their output on television than anywhere else. They're beguiled by the glamour too. Sometimes a compromise is reached. Part of the advertising budget is put into TV, part into print. Oh, what sins are committed under the nice-guy guise of compromise!

But it isn't only those who are enamoured of TV who make Common Advertising Mistake #3. Advertising agencies in their eagerness to get an account often exaggerate, and never underestimate, what the advertising dollars budgeted by the client can accomplish. If one agency says four million people can be influenced with $300,000, and a competing agency says five million people can be influenced with the same amount, the advertiser is likely to choose the agency that promises more.

Common Mistake #3: Trying to do too much with too few advertising dollars.

The procedure for avoiding this mistake is closely allied to the procedure for avoiding **Common Mistake #4: The advertiser doing too much of the agency's work.**

Most people outside the advertising agencies don't realize the vast facilities any good agency possesses for selecting media.

One source, for example, gives the media analyst circulation figures for hundreds of magazines. Another source gives him readerships, which are not the same as circulations. Circulation is the number of copies that are printed and distributed. Since more than one person on the average may read some copies, the readership figures are higher. For some publications the figure is a little higher; for others the readership is a multiple of the circulation.

A third source gives the media analyst facts on how well the advertisements in a specific magazine are read. Readers of some magazines pay more attention to the advertisements than do others. The analyst may also have information on how well readers of specific magazines respond—which does not necessarily correlate with how much attention readers pay to the advertisements.

The point is agencies are so much better equipped to scientifically select media that it is not advisable for the advertiser to make any suggestions until after he has heard what the agency proposes.

Some advertisers go even further in doing the agency's work—they write the advertisements. They reason that since they know so much more about their product or service or company, it is easier for them to do it than to explain to the agency what they want. They lose a precious asset possessed only by the agency: objectivity. The agency can see the advertiser from the outside. Its people are better situated to put themselves in the place of those the advertising messages are aimed at.

The advertiser can avoid Common Advertising Mistakes #3 and #4 in several ways. First, by defining what he wants the advertising to accomplish. Second, by refraining from telling the agency how it should accomplish those objectives. Third, by telling the agency that an objective evaluation of the effectiveness of the advertising will be established. And fourth, by using whatever knowledge of advertising he has to cross-question the agency after it presents its media and creative recommendations.

23

ITT wanted to be better known and more highly regarded. For this purpose, the company budgeted $5 million in a single year for television, magazine, newspaper, and radio advertising. Television necessarily took the bulk of the budget—$4 million. Six commercials were made, one of which is shown opposite. On the next page, a newspaper advertisement is also shown. Full pages were used in magazines, one-third pages in newspapers. In the calendar year, awareness increased 56 percent. The number of people who confused ITT with AT&T was cut in half. And the positive characteristics cited in the advertising were more strongly associated with ITT. These were the results of a telephone survey made of over 1,500 households with annual incomes of $15,000 or more. (In a properly conducted survey of this kind, 1,500 is a large enough sample to be considered reliable.) The company and the agency, Needham, Harper & Steers, won an award from the American Marketing Association for this campaign, largely on the basis of these results. Note the use of specific ways in which ITT actually helps people and society. Note the broad appeal of the openings of both the commercial and the ad: ". . . the tracks and trains are like nowhere else." And ". . . another heart attack." Note the interesting and convincing way the story is told in each instance. On TV, the whizzing trains added much to the commercial's effectiveness. Note that the commercial gets ITT into the story early but naturally. The advertisement doesn't need to repeat the name in the copy because the logo is tastefully prominent.

WITH A BUDGET OF LESS THAN $2 MILLION

Small packages are traditionally shipped on passenger planes when airmail is too slow or uncertain. Federal Express was formed for the specific purpose of providing door-to-door shipment on an airline devoted solely to delivering small packages. It was up to the advertising to communicate these advantages to shippers.

In a large company the decision on which freight forwarder to use may be made by anyone from a clerk in the mailroom to the president. And it is often not a conscious decision, because the company tends to use the forwarder it has always used. TV was desirable as a medium for two reasons: its intrusive quality and its coverage of all levels of management. Television, however, suffers from brevity. In addition, the company wanted direct responses. A combined TV and print campaign was indicated, but the budget was too small for national coverage—close to but less than $2 million was available for both space

ITT

"CORECT": 60

PRODUCT: CONTINUOUS REMOTE CONTROL OF TRAINS

ANNCR (VOICE OVER): Between Hamburg and Bremen in Germany, the tracks and trains are like nowhere else.

SOUND: ROAR OF HIGH-SPEED TRAIN DOWN TRACK.

Here, the tracks talk to the trains and the trains talk to the tracks.

Tracks and trains talk to each other

in a computer-based control system, created by the people at ITT. It's being tested by the German railways.

In the ITT system, the train continuously reports its speed and location.

And if there's another train ahead, the track tells it to slow down—

or even stops it automatically. SOUND: TRAIN STOPS. AFTER INTERVAL, STARTS DOWN TRACK AGAIN.

When this ITT system reaches our part of the world, trains will be able to run more often

safely—on whatever line you take.

And go a lot faster too, as they talk their way down the tracks...

ITT

The best ideas are the ideas that help people.

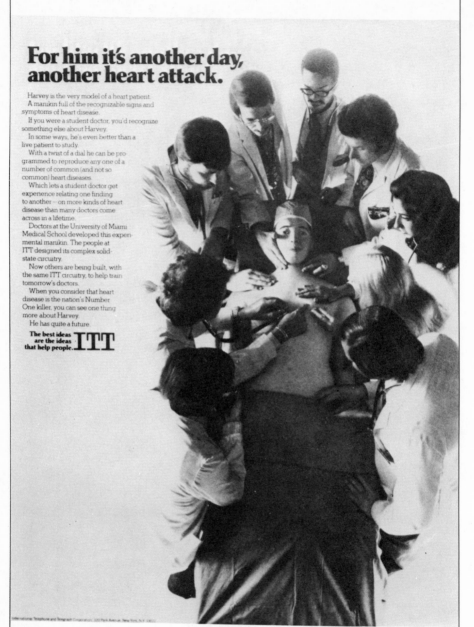

For him it's another day, another heart attack.

Harvey is the very model of a heart patient. A manikin full of the recognizable signs and symptoms of heart disease.

If you were a student doctor, you'd recognize something else about Harvey.

In some ways, he's even better than a live patient to study.

With a twist of a dial he can be programmed to reproduce any one of a number of common (and not so common) heart diseases.

Which lets a student doctor get experience relating one finding to another — on more kinds of heart disease than many doctors come across in a lifetime.

Doctors at the University of Miami Medical School developed this experimental manikin. The people at ITT designed its complex solid-state circuitry.

Now others are being built, with the same ITT circuitry, to help train tomorrow's doctors.

When you consider that heart disease is the nation's Number One killer, you can see one thing more about Harvey.

He has quite a future.

The best ideas are the ideas that help people. ITT

and time in Federal Express's third year of operation. Carl Ally Inc., the advertising agency, recommended spot TV concentrated in markets with the greatest potential, plus newspaper and newsweekly advertisements. Advertising was also placed in the Yellow Pages, and a direct mail campaign was undertaken.

One of their typical commercials is shown below. Note how emotion is immediately aroused in a viewer concerned with shipping by reminding him of a mishap that has occurred or that could occur to something he himself has shipped. The rest of the commercial proves how easily this error can be corrected by Federal Express—and how difficult it could be to correct if the packages were shipped by a competitor. Note the specific mention of the passenger airlines for clarity.

FEDERAL EXPRESS TV COMMERCIAL

Video	Audio
1. MAN IN FRONT OF FEDERAL EXPRESS TRUCK.	MAN: If Federal Express misplaces a package,
2. OPENS DOORS TO TRUCK TO REVEAL INSIDE.	there's only a few places it can be. For instance, here in one of our trucks,
3. CUT TO SAME MAN BEFORE A FEDERAL EXPRESS PLANE. DOLLY BACK TO REVEAL TRUCK AND PLANE TOGETHER.	or here, in one of our own planes. If one of our competitors misplaces a package, it's either on his truck, or on American, United, TWA, Braniff, Continental, Eastern, PSA, Western, National .
4. CUT TO LOGO: "FEDERAL EXPRESS. TAKE AWAY OUR PLANES, AND WE'D BE JUST LIKE EVERYBODY ELSE."	(FADES OUT)

By the end of the year, a study showed that Federal Express had become first in awareness among all air freight forwarders, and its slogan the best recognized slogan of any freight forwarder. More important, while revenues of the freight forwarding industry increased only 5 percent that year, Federal Express revenues increased a big 70 percent. Its share of the market climbed from 13.2 percent to 21.3 percent.

6

BEING CHEAP
CAN BE EXPENSIVE

At the other end of the spectrum from the TV Splurger is the advertiser who makes a different kind of mistake. He looks for a cheap medium—one where the page rate or the line rate is low. He advertises in a suburban newspaper rather than the metropolitan daily covering the same and contiguous areas, not because his business is in that suburb, but because the cost of each ad is so much less. Or he advertises in a specialty magazine—not because the audience he wants to reach coincides with the readers of the magazine, but because its page rate is low.

If he wants direct response—and most advertisers of this type do—he is apt to be disappointed in the returns, and he will decide that advertising is not for him.

He has made **Common Mistake #5: Choosing a medium based on its low rate rather than on its cost per thousand readers, listeners, or viewers.**

Publications and other media with large audiences are generally more efficient for the advertiser than those with smaller audiences.

Why this is generally true can be seen by considering magazines. There is a relatively high fixed cost in publishing a magazine—in typography and printing costs, editorial salaries, management, and other overhead. Additional copies cost very little more to print and distribute. The larger the circulation, the lower the cost per issue. Smaller magazines must therefore get more income per issue from advertisers and/or subscribers. What is more, editors and writers for smaller magazines are usually paid less. And if the editors and writers are paid less, what the reader and the advertiser get for their money may be of relatively lower quality. The magazine with the bigger circulation has the capability of being more efficient.

HOW OFTEN?

For some reason, advertisers who wrongly insist on imitating package goods advertising usually ignore the very quality that makes it work — repetition.

No matter how ingenious a package goods commercial may be, it cannot be effective unless it is repeated often. The more often a viewer sees a commercial, the more likely he is to remember both the brand name and its favorable connotations.

Advertisers don't advertise frequently enough for several reasons. They may want to stretch their advertising dollars over a longer period of time. They know how obnoxious repetition can become and they don't want their advertising to be obnoxious. They may be poorly advised by their advertising agencies. They may decide themselves how often they want their advertising to run, instead of asking the agency's opinion. They may like big advertisements, and so sacrifice frequency for size. Finally, they may not realize that only a percentage, often only a small percentage, of the audience actually sees each commercial or ad, no matter how brilliant it may be.

Common Mistake #6: Not advertising frequently enough.

Not that all types of advertising benefit from frequent repetition. Some advertisers ignore package goods frequency, and they should. These are the direct response advertisers.

Experience shows that direct response advertisements should be spaced out for maximum effectiveness. How many days, weeks, or months should elapse between ads depends on a number of factors, one of which is the size of the advertisement.

Let's consider a full-page direct response advertisement in *The New York Times* — not unusual for, say, mail order health insurance. An advertisement of this size, presuming it is well written and well designed, will on its first appearance be read by a large percentage of the regular readers of the *Times* — and will bring replies from a percentage of that percentage.

If the advertisement were repeated the next day, the responses would drop drastically. On the first day, the ad would have drawn responses from most of those readers who were apt to respond at all. Responses on the second day would come principally from those who had not seen it before, or who had seen it but were more receptive the second day. In short, repeating a direct response advertisement does not have the same beneficial effect on sales that repeating a package goods commercial does, because the marketing method is different.

A single package goods commercial is usually ineffective because the brand name must be seen again and again if it is to be remembered by viewers. A single direct response advertisement must pay for itself.

This matter of frequency is complicated for *all* kinds of advertising. As we have seen, the size of the advertisement or the length of the commercial makes a difference. The character of the product or service also makes a difference. So does the type of medium — TV, radio, newspapers, magazines, billboards, car cards, direct mail — and even the specific medium within each type.

How can the advertiser and the agency decide on the correct frequency? By studying past successes for products and services that are marketed in the same way. And by measuring the results of that advertising and adjusting their own schedule accordingly.

MORE ABOUT
FREQUENCY

Question: How does the size of the advertisement affect the frequency?

Answer: Since small advertisements reach only a small percentage of readers, they must appear more often in order to achieve the same impression. But the ratio between size and frequency is not constant. Studies of newspaper advertisments show that, on the average, both readership and responses increase as the size of the advertisement increases. A full page, however, will not get twice as much attention as a half page. It's common sense. A half-page advertisement will usually be noticed by such a high percentage of readers that it would be impossible to double readership. On the other hand, a single column ad a couple of inches deep will attract the attention of such a small percentage of readers that doubling its size is likely to double its readership. We'll have more on this in the next chapter.

Question: Does this same logic hold for radio and television?

Answer: More or less. Thirty-second commercials are actually *more* than half as memorable as one-minute commercials and are therefore more economical if the objective is to increase awareness. If direct responses are the objective, however, the results from radio differ somewhat from those you can expect from print.

In print, if several advertisements run within a short time, the second ad will pull fewer responses than the first, the third fewer than the second, and so on. The trick in placing direct response advertisements is to discover how closely they can be spaced so that later ads will pull nearly as much as earlier ones. The reason is this: A well-written and well-designed direct response ad is read by and affects a very high percentage of its audience the first time it appears. When it appears the second time, fewer readers are left to be affected. As time goes on, however, the publication gains other readers. In addition, readers' attitudes and needs change, so that after a certain length of time a second advertisement with the same offer will pull as well, or nearly as well, as the first. The time span can range from a few days to a year or more, depending on the publication and other factors.

In radio, however, experience indicates that the opposite is true. The second radio commercial usually pulls more responses than the first, and the third more than the second. This is because the listener, unlike the reader, cannot ask for an instant replay. If he doesn't quite understand the advertiser's offer, or if he doesn't remember the address or telephone number, he doesn't respond. But if the commercial arouses his interest the first time, he will listen attentively the second or third time and he will then be more likely to respond.

Question: How does the character of the product or service affect the frequency?

Answer: In somewhat the same way size does. Readership statistics show that some products and services — life insurance, for example — hold low interest for readers; others, such as automobiles, arouse high interest. To obtain the same results, an insurance campaign would have to have a higher frequency than an automobile campaign. The character of the product or service is so important, in fact, that the most popular readership service groups ads by industry, so that advertising people can make valid comparisons.

HOW BIG?

For both economic and emotional reasons, nearly everybody involved in creating and placing an advertising campaign would like print advertisements to be larger than they should be.

The copywriter likes a big ad for the freedom it gives him, because his words will generally be in big type, because his friends are more likely to see and comment on the ad, and because small ads don't win awards.

The art director prefers a big ad for similar reasons.

The owners of the advertising agency prefer big ads because creative costs are the same as for small ads but commissions are higher. Account executives and account supervisors like them because big ads can be dramatic, and are easier to sell. Advertisers like big ads because they can feel proud – of the advertisement, of the company, and of themselves. Some agencies even show blown-up versions of the ads they are recommending because they know that the larger the size the greater the emotional response on the part of the client.

And finally, owners of publications and their salespeople prefer big ads for the same reason a car salesman would rather sell a Cadillac than a Chevrolet.

Common Mistake #7: Making the advertisement bigger than it need be.

There is evidence, not widely known, that the most economical size for a newspaper advertisement is one that just dominates the page. A little thought shows why this is so. As the reader turns the page, looking for news, his eye is most likely to be attracted to the largest advertisement on the page (presuming the ads are equally well done). Some readers may look at the other ads, but a good number will not. The dominating advertisement thus gets a bonus in readership. If the advertisement is any bigger than the dominating size, it attracts more readers, but not in proportion to the increase in size. If the advertisement is just less than the dominating size, the drop in readership is likely to be disproportionately great.

Decisions regarding the size of a newspaper advertisement, however, are seldom governed by the principle of dominating size. More often, the biggest influence is the competition. The agency and/or the advertiser may have the attitude, "We don't know what size the ad should be. Maybe the competition does. We can't go far wrong by doing what the competition is doing."

The lower the position of the person making the decision, whether at the agency or at the client, the more prevalent the do-as-the-competition-does syndrome. The essence of bureaucratic survival is to avoid criticism. If the advertisements are bigger than the competition's, the criticism can be "Wasteful!" If the ads are smaller, the decision maker is accepting second place for his company.

When do-as-the-competition-does is combined with even-unit thinking (full page, half-page, quarter-page), the result is a page full of advertisements of the same size. This is particularly prevalent in *The Wall Street Journal*, where quarter-page advertisements are common. Any *Wall Street Journal* advertiser who uses just a few lines more than a quarter page gets a big bonus in attention.

There are valid reasons, however, for making a newspaper advertisement larger or smaller than the dominating size. It may be wise to increase the size if the subject requires the importance of the full page. Or if the number of words is great, and/or the illustrations are large or there are many of them. Or if it is important to impress the reader with the size of the company. Studies show that readers tend to equate the size of the advertisement with the size of the company. They assume that small companies place small advertisements, and that large companies place large advertisements. And they are not far wrong.

There are also valid reasons for making a newspaper advertisement smaller than the dominating size. The budget may be too small. On a fixed budget, there is an inverse relationship between the size of the advertisement and the frequency. And it's generally more effective to give the nod to frequency. The nature of the product may be such that an increase in size will hardly increase readership by the target audience. Consider, for example, shoes for men with feet so wide they cannot buy what they need in the usual shoe store. There are a limited number of men with such feet and no newspaper is read by a sufficient number of them to justify the cost of a large ad. But these men are so anxious to get proper fitting shoes that small ads can pull in enough responses to make the ads pay.

Similar logic holds for magazine advertising, but not to the same extent. The most economical size generally is two-thirds of a page. This size gets almost as much attention as a full page, and it costs much less. However, in some publications full pages get better positions than two-thirds pages. The big error advertisers make is the unnecessary use of the double-page spread; on the average, readership is usually less than double that for a single page. Much better results can usually be obtained by using two single pages in different issues at a fractionally greater cost.

In broadcast, the same problems don't arise. Thirty-second TV commercials are now standard. As a way to increase awareness, they have been shown to be more economical than one-minute commercials. TV costs are so enormous that everybody is cost-conscious, so it's seldom that longer commercials are used.

Less information can be communicated over the radio in thirty seconds than through TV, because radio relies on only one of our senses—hearing. The name of what is being advertised needs to be repeated if it is to be remembered. Since the cost of radio is comparatively low, one-minute radio commercials are usually the sensible choice.

FRACTIONAL-PAGE ADS SUCCEED IN COMPETITION WITH MULTI-MILLION-DOLLAR TV

Tylenol was just another in a long list of drugs supplied to drug stores by the McNeil Laboratories division of Johnson & Johnson. Then a low-budget print campaign was undertaken in trade publications such as the *Medical News Times* and *The Apothecary*. The purpose of the advertising was to cause doctors and druggists to recommend Tylenol. A routine approach would have been to feature headlines

Tylenol or aspirin

---

which analgesic for the ulcer patient?

"Aspirin...plays a significant part in exacerbation of ulcer symptoms and is at least a contributory cause in one in eight cases of haematemesis...."[1]

Acetaminophen "...should therefore be used in preference to aspirin as a pure analgesic in all cases of peptic ulcer."[2]

Aspirin not only may irritate an existing ulcer condition, but also may be a causal or precipitating factor to ulceration. So when a customer has—or has had—an ulcer, be sure the headache remedy he buys from you is TYLENOL...not aspirin or aspirin-containing compounds.

Precautions and Adverse Reactions: If a rare sensitivity reaction occurs, the drug should be stopped. TYLENOL has rarely been found to produce any side effects, such as gastric discomfort.

References: 1. Muir, A., and Cossar, I. A.: Brit. Med. J. 2:7-12 (July 2) 1955. 2. Craddock, D.: Practitioner 189:192-200 (Aug.) 1962.
Supplied: scored, white tablets of 325 mg. in packages of 12, 24 and 100.

safer than aspirin, yet just as effective for the relief of pain

Tylenol (acetaminophen)

McNeil Laboratories, Inc., Fort Washington, Pennsylvania 19034

that promised a benefit to users of the drug. Instead, Tylenol and aspirin were compared directly in the headline. The comparison was followed by a description of a patient or a condition for which Tylenol was likely to prove superior. The copy then convinced readers of that superiority. So simple and direct that it seems artless, this campaign of fractional print ads, costing less than $100,000 annually in its early years, nevertheless steadily increased sales of Tylenol. Ten years later, Tylenol had captured 10 percent of the $440,000,000 analgesic market. The agency was Kallir, Philips, Ross, Inc.

CREATIVITY IS ALL
—OR IS IT?

Discussions of media selection, frequency, and size are the dullest parts of an advertising presentation. The advertiser is eager to see the commercials or advertisements the agency has prepared, and the agency is eager to show them. The attitude is likely to be, "These advertisements are so brilliant, everyone will not only notice them, read them, and be affected by them, but everyone will talk about them for weeks. So all those petty considerations based on 'other things being equal' have little bearing."

What makes this feeling hard to combat is that it is often true for a single advertisement. Many large advertisements, for example, are so poorly written and designed that it's often easy to beat them with a smaller advertisement that is not necessarily brilliant, just creatively competent. But it's seldom that a whole campaign can consist of advertisements with every one so brilliant they can make up for deficiencies in size or frequency.

Depending on creativity to make up for, say, too little frequency is like going into a football game with only nine players. It may be possible for nine football stars to beat eleven ordinary players, but would you bet on it? The eleven players may turn out to be stars too.

Common Mistake #8: Expecting too much from creativity in copy and art.

It can be avoided by basing media decisions on the averages and by treating above-average results from copy and art as a bonus. Remember that most other advertisers think their advertising is above average, too. And yet only half of all advertising can be above average.

11

BEWARE OF
IMITATIONS

An influential executive within a company sees another company's advertising that he likes. If it's a print ad, he tears it out. If it's a commercial, he describes it. And he sends the ad or the description to his advertising department, or to the advertising agency, or he shows it to the chief executive officer or the board of directors—each time with the comment, "Why can't we have advertising like this!"

He has just committed **Common Mistake #9: Imitating instead of analyzing.**

This mistake occurs often because, more than most of us care to admit, we base our actions, our words, even our thoughts, on what others do. It's the earliest and easiest form of learning; it's how we learn to speak, for example. Civilization, in fact, is largely based on imitation. One generation learns how to achieve a desirable result and successive generations imitate those actions. In moving into a new job, we are shown, or we ask, how it was done before. And why not? There's no point, as the cliché goes, in reinventing the wheel. It would, in fact, be impossible for any of us to get anything done within a reasonable length of time if we did not imitate the ways in which others dress, shave, drive, eat, and so on.

Imitating is also the *safest* course of action—in school, in business, and in the army. The pupil, executive, or soldier who does things the way they've always been done can't be criticized.

Imitation, however, can be the most dangerous course of action for an advertising director, copywriter, art director, or media analyst — for anybody responsible for advertising. Every advertising situation is different. No two companies have exactly the same marketing program, or the same advantages.

Ads that are held up as examples for the company to follow may be wrong for one or more reasons. Consider these situations.

The admired ad is a television commercial — but TV is an inefficient way to reach the company's target audience. Or it's a full-page ad — but smaller ads with greater frequency are more effective for the company. Or it's in full color — whereas newspapers are the appropriate medium. Or it's humorous — but humor would be wrong for the company. Finally, the admired ad is mostly a human interest illustration with short copy — but the company's advertising requires longer copy and factual illustrations, if any.

These wrongly admired ads are the bane of every competent advertising person's existence. Copywriters and art directors who won't produce advertising "like the kind I just showed you" are termed prima donnas. Account executives who resist are looked on as "uncooperative."

Yet many "creative" people are guilty of the sin of imitation. Art directors copy layouts from ads they admire, even though often the layout is not functionally correct for the ad they are working on. Copywriters give a fresh twist to a well-known slogan — reminding audiences of the original instead of increasing awareness of the product they're being paid to promote.

It's not even safe to imitate advertisements in the same industry or category. First, because imitative advertising may remind prospects of the competition — and may even help sell their brand. Second, because even within categories, or within industries, the advertising requirements are different for each company, product, or service.

Industrial advertising, for example, can take any of several forms. If the company wants to pave the way for salesmen's calls, the advertising must create an image and be memorable. A dominant illustration and short copy may therefore be appropriate, and high frequency important. If, on the other hand, the company wants to get leads for salesmen, the advertising may stress what is being offered (a free booklet, for example) instead of the company itself or its products. Here, long copy may be appropriate, and frequency unimportant.

As a matter of fact, the accepted categories of advertising, such as *package goods, direct response, industrial, retail, classified, au-*

tomobile, are misleading and often overlapping. It is not possible to take one category and set up a body of advertising principles for it. Tylenol and Virginia Slims, for example, are both package goods, but look at the difference in their advertising!

It would be more sensible to set up categories in terms of what the advertising is expected to accomplish, such as:

1. Get action immediately.
2. Get action within the next few days.
3. Cause the target audience to choose the advertised brand.
4. Cause the prospect to recognize the brand or company name.
5. Prevent a specific action.

But even these categories would be insufficient, as you will see. There a host of other factors, such as the nature of the target audience and the size of the budget, all of which can make important differences.

Analysis of the company's advertising requirements is therefore essential. So is a knowledge of what has worked and what has failed in a variety of advertising categories. In the next several chapters the tools and knowledge necessary for analysis are supplied so that successful advertising can be created and placed.

12

THE FOUR COMMONEST
MISTAKES IN
LAYOUT AND ART

An advertisement needs artists for its creation, but it is not necessarily Art in the sense that a painting is. An advertisement does not exist to be appreciated for its own sake, but to influence the actions of its readers. This action may be immediate as with direct response advertisements, delayed a day or so as with package goods commercials, or delayed much longer as with attitude-changing campaigns. Why should a corporation pay good money for advertising unless it results in actions beneficial to the corporation sooner or later?

This is why nearly all advertising awards are nonsense — why there is no correlation, direct or inverse, between winning awards and effectiveness. Award-winning advertisements are generally beautiful and entertaining. The fact is that an ugly advertisement, even an ad that is repulsive to some readers, can be very effective.

To repeat: the chief function of an art director is not to create a beautiful advertisement, but to design one that will gain the attention of a large number of readers. There are no hard and fast rules for him to follow, but there are untold numbers of studies that show where the pitfalls lie, such as:

Using fancy drawings. Photographs and realistic art usually gain more attention than drawings or paintings and are more convincing. Readers accept photographs as objective, as picturing what is real. There is no distortion of the truth by a third party. But art directors like artwork because they can distort. Artwork allows greater opportunity for the exercise of style, for subjectivity, for communicating the viewpoint of the artist toward the subject.

This is not to say that artwork should never be used in an advertisement. If arousing a certain kind of feeling is of paramount importance, and can only be accomplished through artwork, then artwork should be used.

In working toward gaining attention, art directors who are advertising men first concentrate on what is *in* the photograph. They may follow certain principles of photography, such as making sure the composition has a center of attention, but they know that it is most important that the *content* of the photograph attract the eye, arouse emotion, and cause the reader to move on to the headline and copy.

Irregular cropping of photographs. Rectangular photographs gain more attention and are more convincing than other shapes, particularly irregular shapes. It is true that a silhouetted photograph, like the one in the ITT ad, may do as well or better without the background under certain circumstances. A background may be distracting, or so cluttered as to confuse the reader. Silhouetting is more common, and is often correctly used in newspaper advertising, because the medium is so coarse that background details may be indiscernible.

Multiple illustrations. Studies show that a single dominant illustration will usually get more attention than multiple illustrations. However, a number of small illustrations scattered throughout the text can increase readership.

Movie ads sometimes feature multiple silhouetted illustrations for a special reason. Movie advertising must arouse the same emotion as the type aroused by the entire two-hour or so film advertised. Experience shows that a single scene from the film will seldom do this; those silhouetted montages so common in movie advertising do it very well. Note that the silhouetted montages are successful because in this kind of advertising communicating a certain emotion is more important than attracting attention — and conviction of truth is extraneous. A rectangular photograph of a well-known star, however, will usually attract attention well.

Art directors who specify artwork instead of photographs simply because they like it, who carve photographs into fancy shapes, who make beautiful designs out of combinations of photographs, or who don't put the principal illustration where it logically belongs are guilty of **Common Mistake #10: Trying to gain attention by being different in form instead of content.** Readers are more interested in what an advertiser has to say than in how he says it.

Many advertisers approve advertisements that depend on form rather than content because they really don't want to say anything. Some advertisers have so little confidence in their product or service that they feel deception is necessary, and yet they don't really want to lie. Readership studies indicate that the reader is seldom fooled.

The advertiser is not to blame for the next most common mistake in art and layout. You've seen double-page spreads in magazines in which the headline runs across both pages but is hard to understand because the page margins in the middle leave a big space between the left and right hand sections of the headline. You've also seen newspaper advertisements with photographs that lack punch or even clarity. These are the results of **Common Mistake #11: Creating for presentations, not for the medium.**

When a double-page advertisement is shown in layout form to the client, naturally there are no big holes in the headline. The ad is shown to the client in a form in which it cannot appear in the magazine. Unbelievable? It happens all the time. The art director is given the dimensions of a double-page spread. He makes a layout that looks good to him in his studio—as if he were creating a work of art that exists for its own sake.

In addition, the account executive who will present the layout is either inexperienced or careless. Or he is too concerned with other matters. Or he is so anxious to please the client that he doesn't review the layout for reproduction problems. And the client doesn't know that the ad cannot be reproduced as it is shown him. He's not supposed to be an advertising expert, so he approves it. When he sees the double-page spread again in more finished form it may or may not look exactly as it will appear in the magazine. If it does, there are still two reasons why he may mistakenly approve it. First, the advertiser is not bothered by the hole in the headline because he's concerned with other aspects of the advertisement. And second, the final version may be approved by someone at a lower level in the corporate hierarchy. The lower-level executive knows the layout was approved at a higher level, so he assumes the headline irregularity was approved. Bureaucracy is the curse of the executive class.

A muddy photograph in a newspaper advertisement is the result of even more subtle errors. Newsprint is a crude printing medium. Any photograph used in newspaper advertising must be mostly black and white, and have very little gray. Otherwise the grays blend with the blacks and the content is hard to discern. But high-contrast photographs don't allow the photographer or the art director much room for artistry, for those fine effects that make them proud of themselves and that are admired by their fellow photographers and art directors. High-contrast photographs are seldom hung in museums.

So the photographer takes, develops, and shows to the agency people a photograph that looks magnificent on high-quality photographic paper. And this photograph is shown to the client who, naturally, thinks it is outstanding. He's not supposed to be an expert on newspaper reproduction.

How can photographs be made to reproduce well in newspapers? There are several ways. (1) Make a high-contrast print. (2) Retouch the photograph heavily. Agencies hesitate to do this if the client is unsophisticated, because the heavily painted photograph looks crude until it is softened by newspaper reproduction. (3) Use a special screen which reduces grays to blacks and whites. These screens give an effect that is halfway between a photograph and artwork. Their power to get attention and convince readers approximates that of a straight photograph.

Common Mistake #12 springs from a psychological attribute that, paradoxically, makes many art directors good at their jobs. Most art directors hate words. It isn't just that they are not much interested in words. They have an active aversion to words.

Alert account executives see objective evidence of this every day. Art directors tend to misspell words in headlines they hand letter. They misspell so often, it cannot be carelessness. It cannot be they do not know how to spell. As anyone with even a layman's understanding of Freudian psychology knows, it is antagonism toward words.

For many art directors, words are simply a part of the design they are assigned to create. Interestingly enough, art directors seldom make the type too small, but some will do just about anything else to make words hard to read. They will put the body copy in reverse — that is, print it in white on black. Studies show that headlines are just about as readable in reverse, but that body copy in reverse is less readable. Or they will print the type over a tint. This is particularly serious in a newspaper. The proof of the advertisement may look fine when the paper is slick, but when the ad appears in the newspaper the tint may be too dark and the words unreadable, even by the mother of the president of the company doing the advertising.

Some art directors will also print body copy over an illustration in a newspaper advertisement. Some of the words are bound to be indecipherable, or nearly so, particularly if the illustration is dark. And there are art directors who will even print the body copy in reverse over an illustration!

They are all committing **Common Mistake #12: Being over-creative with type.** This mistake doesn't just reduce readership. It makes those who do read the advertisement feel, often rightly, that the advertiser doesn't feel strongly about what the advertisement says. It decreases the advertisement's convincing power.

Common Mistake #13 has to do with the advertising company's name. Generally, advertisers feel the bigger the logo the better. But the art director is usually a long distance away from the company people, separated from them by the Account Supervisor, the Account Executive, and perhaps his group head or the Creative Director. He often sees the company's name as an intrusion. Did Utrillo sign his paintings in big black type?

The size of the company's logo is often a compromise, arrived at after a tug-of-war between the account people who know what the client wants and the art director who knows what is esthetically pleasing.

The truth is, a big logo is right for some kinds of advertising, wrong for others. The size of the logo should be determined primarily by the purpose of the advertising, but is instead often determined by the personalities of the several people involved, resulting in **Common Mistake #13: Making the logo the wrong size.**

In direct response advertising, the company's name should usually be small, probably no bigger than the body copy. The success of a direct response advertisement depends largely on the headline and how strongly it appeals to readers' needs and desires. There is only one possible reason for making the advertiser's name bigger than the body copy: When the company's name is already well known and highly regarded, making it larger than the body copy may make the headline promise more believable, and may therefore increase returns.

In image advertising, the purpose is to increase awareness of the company's name and improve the attitude of the target audience toward the company. Isn't it obvious, therefore, that the company's name should be big? As big—or nearly as big—as the headline type? So why do image advertisements appear so often in *Fortune* or elsewhere with the company's name in small type?

Partly because of the predilections of art directors. And partly because account executives fail to explain to advertisers the rationale behind the size of the company's name. Many an advertiser doesn't realize that only a small percentage of the readers of the magazine will read all the copy in his advertisement. None of his professional advisers have told him this. No one has said, "About seven times as many people will read the headline of your advertisement as will read the body copy." If your logo is as big, or nearly as big, as the headline, studies show that those who read the headline will also correctly associate your company with what it says.

Many an advertiser looks on the image advertising for his firm as an extension of himself—and, if he is a strong chief executive officer or the owner, it is. When he is shown an image ad with the company's name in small type, he may appreciate how tasteful the ad is, and further realize that increasing the size of the company's name would destroy the balance between the elements of the advertisement. He falls into the trap of judging the advertisement in the same way he judged the paintings that hang in his office. The company's name can be small in an image advertisement when it appears in the headline. Then the logo can be left out entirely, giving the advertisement an editorial look which generally gets good readership. In straight product or service advertising, however, most successful advertisers put the name of the product or service being offered in big type. (See the Parker Pen ad for an extreme example.)

If all the people involved in creating and approving advertisements judge the size of the company's name by asking "How much will communicating the name of the product or company to the reader affect the results?" it is likely that the size will not be far wrong. What is more, there will be a rational basis for adjusting disagreements.

A QUALITY IMAGE KEEPS PARKER ON TOP

By an overwhelming margin, Parker Pen is the most preferred gift pen throughout the country. The advertising mission, therefore, is to cause those who buy the gift to feel that those who receive it will recognize its worth. Since there is very little difference in the writing

PARKER 75

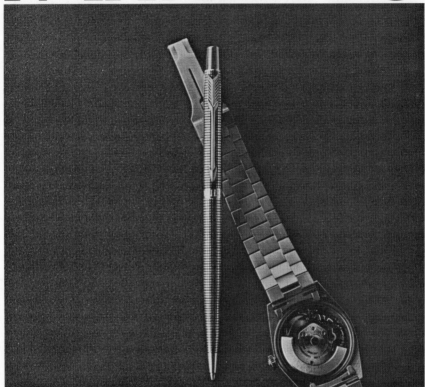

Rolex Oyster Perpetual Day-Date Chronometer in 18K Gold. Parker 75 Classic Ball Pen in solid sterling silver.

No part of this $2,800 watch is made more precisely than the point of a Parker 75 Classic Ball Pen.

The point of a Parker 75 Classic Ball Pen is not large. Fifty points, side by side, measure one inch.

For this pen to write the way we want it to—clean, crisp, without skip or blob —the point must be as near a perfect sphere as we can make it.

Though we take three weeks to make the point, perfection escapes us.

We can, however, come close. We allow a maximum deviation of ten-millionths of an inch in its sphericity. We are equally demanding but less

successful in controlling the diameter. A given batch of balls may vary from another of the same point size by plus or minus 100 millionths of an inch.

The stainless steel socket in which our point turns must also be very true. Into the medium ball point socket, for example, we put six channels, each about four-thousandths of an inch in width and depth. Through these the ink moves to the point.

The interesting thing about all this is we take this trouble with the

disposable parts of the 75 Classic Ball Pen. These are all parts of the refill cartridge.

Needless to say, we worry as much, if not more so, about those parts you keep.

The Parker 75 Classic Ball Pen. Though it's made up of approximations, it does make a very nice gift.

✦ PARKER
World's most wanted pens

Parker 75 Classic Ball Pens from $5 to $450. Matching pencils. Ample engraving area for full monogram.

qualities of pens, it would be very difficult to communicate the superiority of the Parker Pen through direct promise of a benefit. The advertising therefore concentrates on the quality of the workmanship, putting the pen in the same class with a very expensive watch. In the black-and-white reproduction of a Parker Pen ad on the preceding page, the effect of quality of the original full color is lost, but note that a square illustration has been used because it gets attention and is convincing. If the pen and the watch were silhouetted, the comparison would seem less realistic and the elegant image would be destroyed. Note the large yet tasteful product name. The advertising, created by J. Walter Thompson, appears in magazines such as *U.S. News & World Report* in order to reach a high-income audience most efficiently. Since Parker switched from TV to print and began promoting the high end of its line in selected consumer magazines, its consolidated sales have more than doubled in four years and now exceed $117 million.

CREATIVITY IN CONTENT, NOT IN FORM

The early award-winning Volkswagen advertisements, which made Volkswagen the largest-selling imported car in the United States in the 1960s, were often called "unconventional" and "daring." The "Lemon" ad was perhaps the most extreme of them all. Note, however, the simplicity of the layout: rectangular photograph, centered headline, type set so it is easy to read. The creativity is in what is said. The straightforward layout makes the advertising believeable and therefore more startling.

The name of the car does not appear in big type in the signature for a sensible reason, not because they wanted to be cute. These advertisements had a tough task to accomplish. Readers in sizable numbers had to be made to consider buying a new, funny-looking foreign car, discover where Volkswagens were sold in their area, and visit a Volkswagen showroom. The principal purpose of the advertising was not — as in package goods and retail advertising — to cause readers to recognize the name when they were in the store, but to *move* readers emotionally and physically. For readers just to associate Volkswagen with some quality such as "sound workmanship" would not have been sufficient. An automobile involves an expenditure of thousands of dollars. People in the market for an automobile had to be

Lemon.

This Volkswagen missed the boat.

The chrome strip on the glove compartment is blemished and must be replaced. Chances are you wouldn't have noticed it; Inspector Kurt Kroner did.

There are 3,389 men at our Wolfsburg factory with only one job: to inspect Volkswagens at each stage of production. (3000 Volkswagens are produced daily; there are more inspectors than cars.)

Every shock absorber is tested (spot checking won't do), every windshield is scanned. VWs have been rejected for surface scratches barely visible to the eye.

Final inspection is really something! VW inspectors run each car off the line onto the Funktionsprüfstand (car test stand), tote up 189 check points, gun ahead to the automatic brake stand, and say "no" to one VW out of fifty.

This preoccupation with detail means the VW lasts longer and requires less mainenance, by and large, than other cars. (It also means a used VW depreciates less than any other car.)

We pluck the lemons; you get the plums.

convinced that The Beetle might be worth all the trouble involved. Headline and signature can breed recognition, but the facts needed to convince readers cannot be compressed into a headline. Eliminating the signature not only piqued curiosity. It also increased readership of the copy by making the ad seem like a friendly communication and not hard sell at all.

The ad ran as a full page in magazines and in approximately one-third of a page in newspapers. A fuller analysis of this Doyle Dane Bernbach campaign follows the chapter on "A New and Complete Theory of Copywriting."

FACTUAL ADVERTISING DRAWS CROWDS

Alexander's depends more than most department stores on advertising to attract shoppers. Several full pages are placed every Sunday and Thursday in the *New York Daily News*, with other ads in *The New York Times*, in suburban newspapers, and on radio. Each ad has a triple purpose: to sell the item (or items) advertised in good quantity, to attract shoppers who will buy not only the item but other merchandise as well, and to communicate the image of Alexander's as an underselling department store. The full-page advertisement on the facing page ran only in the tabloid Sunday *Daily News* in August 1977. In the next two days, 868 blouses were sold. Alexander's estimates that without the promotion only about 100 would have been sold. In other words, this advertisement profitably attracted several hundred shoppers who would not have otherwise visited Alexander's. Note the use of a photograph, not art, so that the reader is convinced that this is exactly what the blouse looks like. Note the shadow behind the figure to further aid reality. To insure good reproduction, high-contrast photography is used, all but a little background eliminated, and the photograph retouched. The highly factual copy reads as follows: "pure silk . . . crepe de chine . . . at a very affordable 19.99 . . . the kind you've seen elsewhere for 2 & 3 times the price! in 7 luscious colors . . .* Vivid teal*Burnished copper*Grape ice*Midnite black*Pearl grey * Tender beige * Snowy white. Pure silk crepe de chine shirts . . . the one thing you can't live without this year . . . especially at this low price." Note the word "affordable" — a superb word choice as it succinctly communicates that this is an expensive item brought down to a reasonable price by Alexander's. Note how the word "luscious"

and the adjective for each color help to remedy the lack of a full-color illustration. The only other non-factual copy reminds the reader that crepe de chine is "in." Copy above the photo identifies Alexander's and tells the days of the sale. Copy below it gives shopping hours for all Alexander's stores and states, "No mail or phone orders," so readers know they have to come to the store. Alexander's, like most retail stores, creates its own newspaper advertising. This is because newspapers, which do not allow commissions to advertising agencies on retail store advertising, charge lower rates for this classification of advertising.

13

FOUR COMMON MISTAKES IN COPY

Let's compare two ads. One features a picture of a man, the other a non-pornographic picture of a woman. Other things being equal, which ad will attract the most readership from men, which from women?

Research has proved, time and again, that the ad featuring the *man* will generally draw more *male* readers, the ad featuring the *woman*, more *female* readers.

There's nothing that so interests people as themselves. As people mature, they learn to conceal this overwhelming concern with themselves, but it's always there. People are born self-centered; it is only training—by parents, institutions, and experience—that causes people to appear to be less self-centered than they are. It's the reason politicians and good salesmen make a point of remembering people's names. It's the reason computer-written letters that include the addressee's name in the body copy as well as in the salutation pull so well. Even though the recipient knows that a computer put his name into type, he still likes the personal recognition and responds positively to it.

For this reason beauty aid advertising is sometimes more effective when it appeals to a woman's love of herself—narcissism—rather than when it appeals to the benefits of appearing attractive to a man.

Yet time and again you'll see advertising that from beginning to

55

end talks about the product, the service, or the company, instead of talking about the reader, viewer, or listener. Time and again image advertisements include the phrase, "We're proud of our. . . ." It is difficult to understand how such language gets into print.

Self-centered bragging never appears in direct response advertising created by experienced advertisers. They know that when an advertisement fails to concentrate on the reader, the returns suffer. In fact, there is a direct relationship between how obvious the results of an advertisement will be and the extent to which it concentrates on the reader. When the results are obvious and immediate, advertisers cannot be self-indulgent and the agency people cannot afford to be sycophants. The Moody's ad following Chapter 3, for example, uses "you" or "your" nine times in the copy. The highly successful Bodine ad at the end of Chapter 15 uses "you" or "your" 27 times.

It cannot be laid down as a rule that the more often "you" appears in an ad the better. Talking directly to the reader may be too obvious when the strategy is to create a certain aura, as for example in the Parker Pen ad a few pages back. It is essential, however, that whatever is in the advertisement be pertinent. A reader who begins to feel, "Why are they telling me all this?" is a reader who turns the page and is lost forever.

Corporate image advertisements, as a class, are the worst offenders, perhaps because most are not objectively measured. The only measure of their effectiveness so far as the advertising agency is concerned is whether the advertiser likes them. So there's always the danger that the agency will submit ads featuring the advertiser instead of the prospective user of the product or service.

Common Mistake #14: Not concentrating the advertising on the reader, listener, or viewer.

It can be avoided by the advertiser realizing how self-centered people really are, by being wary of advertising submitted by the agency that appeals to the egos of company officers, and by establishing objective ways of measuring advertising effectiveness.

Many advertisers make an even bigger mistake—**Common Mistake #15: Making fun of the prospect.** The most usual way is to lampoon a prospective user of the product or service in a cartoon.

We all learn to take a joke on ourselves in good style—but the truth is nobody likes to be laughed at, unless he's got a peculiar masochistic neurosis.

Advertisements that ridicule prospective users appear so often partly because they are clever, do attract attention, and also perhaps allow the advertiser to vent a repressed hate. We all feel some animosity toward those who have power over us. And there's nobody who has as much power over a businessman as a person who on one whim or another may decide to use or not to use the advertiser's product or service.

Note that ads making the *advertiser* ridiculous seldom appear. This is partly because only a foolhardy advertising agency, or a very secure one, would submit an ad that makes fun of those who judge the advertising and who control the purse strings. Yet advertising of this kind could be effective.

A third common mistake in copy derives from the desire of the advertiser to have "clever" copy and by the advertising agency taking the easy way to provide it. **Common Mistake #16: Using a pun in the headline.** A pun is the lowest form of humor. Often readers don't get the joke. More important, a pun necessarily confuses the reader. He thinks the word means one thing, but on second thought realizes it means something else. He then laughs. If the pun is tied in with the advertiser's product, service, or company—or with a promised benefit—the reader or listener is at first confused about the product, service, company, or benefit, and then laughs. Is that desirable? Wouldn't it be better for the reader to clearly understand what is being said and to take the product, service, company, or benefit seriously?

Has any advertising featuring a pun been a proven success, or even won an award? Considerable searching revealed only one—the L'eggs campaign that will be discussed later. In the case of L'eggs, the pun does not confuse the reader, but instead makes clear the relationship between the package and the product. It is the exception that tests the rule.

If you're beginning to believe that it's dangerous to try to be humorous in advertising, you're right. In fact, it is dangerous to be entertaining, especially if the entertainment is excellently done. The viewer, listener, or reader is likely to remember the entertainment and forget what is being advertised.

Advertising agency people love entertaining commercials. Many are frustrated playwrights or producers or actors. Often they are not sales or business oriented, strange to say. They may, in fact, hate business. They see the sales message as a necessary evil, put in the commercial to please the guy who's paying the bill. And the advertiser is often caught up in the same spirit, the glamour of show business. As a consequence, the commercial may be widely admired and remembered, but few viewers remember the advertiser's name or message. How many times has one of your friends described "a great commercial," but couldn't remember the name of the brand or the company?

Common Mistake #17: Entertaining instead of selling.

14

HOW TO GET PEOPLE
TO DO WHAT YOU WANT
WITH WORDS AND PICTURES

An animal learns in two ways. First, through identification: The cub sees what the mature animal does and does not do, and follows his example. He *identifies* with the other animal. Second, through promises: The trainer causes the animal to do what he wants by holding out the hope of food or punishment. No one has figured out any other way of influencing the behavior of an animal, even an animal as sophisticated as man.

It is easier to influence the behavior of men and women because of language. An animal must engage in random behavior in order to discover what he must do in order to gain the promised benefit. Men and women can appreciate what is required in seconds. An animal can only imitate what it sees and hears, while the wonders of language and the facility of the human mind make it possible for men and women to identify with an ideal and understand a promise.

Shakespeare, that master of audience communication, shows how to do it. Here's Henry Tudor, just before the key battle in *Richard III*, promising his troops just about all they could ever hope for:

If you do fight against your country's foes,
Your country's fat shall pay your pains the hire;
If you do fight in safeguard of your wives,
Your wives shall welcome home the conquerors;
If you do free your children from the sword,
Your children's children quit it in your age.

Look at the promises: money, love, a better life for their children! What life insurance copy Shakespeare could have written!

Advertising deals with more mundane matters, but the same emotion must be aroused: hope of a better life. The promise may be of something superior: "Get clothes whiter than white." Or something more: "Get four for the price of three." Or something cheaper: "Lowest fares to Europe."

The most successful promises aim directly at the audience's self-interest, the more physical the better: taste, comfort, easier life, health, security, the chance to save time, the chance to save or make money, pleasure, power, greater sexual attractiveness. And the promise is backed up by logic. The formula is: "To get what you want, do what I want." The technique is cerebral.

The identification technique is quite different. It need not be logical. It does not depend upon reason for success but upon instinct. It aims at the heart, not the brain.

Another example from Shakespeare may help make the technique clear. Here is Henry V to his men just before the battle of Agincourt. Note that Henry V even uses the word "imitate," and suggests identification with admirable animals and the audience's fathers and mothers. The emotional appeal is to pride – and there's hardly any logic to it at all.

> ... But when the blast of war blows in our ears,
> Then imitate the action of the tiger;
> Stiffen the sinews, summon up the blood,
> Disguise fair nature with hard-favour'd rage;
> Then lend the eye a terrible aspect;
> Let it pry through the portage of the head
> Like the brass cannon ...
> On, on, you noble English,
> Whose blood is fet from fathers of war-proof! –
> Fathers that, like so many Alexanders,
> Have in these parts from morn till even fought,
> And sheath'd their swords for lack of argument: –
> Dishonour not your mothers, now attest
> That those whom you call'd fathers did beget you!
> Be copy now to men of grosser blood,
> And teach them how to war! – And you, good yeomen,
> Whose limbs were made in England, show us here

The mettle of your pasture; let us swear
That you are worth your breeding: which I doubt not;
For there is none of you so mean and base,
That hath not noble lustre in your eyes.
I see you stand like greyhounds in the slips,
Straining upon the start. The game's afoot:
Follow your spirit; and upon this charge
Cry—God for Harry! England! and Saint George!"

Ideals change, but the fundamental technique remains the same. Marlboro became the leading cigarette brand by causing smokers to identify with the masculine cowboy. Virginia Slims became a big seller by associating itself with the women's liberation movement— "You've come a long way, baby!" (See the advertisement in the next chapter.) The U.S. Marines modernized Henry V in billboards showing good-looking young Marines in their distinctive dress uniforms and the words: "We're looking for a few good men."

But sometimes identification advertising is not that obvious. The ITT commercial and ad at the end of Chapter 5 also use identification. They try to make their audiences feel that ITT is doing what a company should be doing, improving conditions for other people. A viewer need never ride nor even intend to ride a train to be influenced by the commercial. A reader need have no worries about a heart attack to be favorably affected by the ad. Audiences are moved toward a feeling that ITT is a socially desirable company, one that belongs in the ideal world with which they'd like to be associated.

Identification is most effective when the advertising does not have to carry the load alone. Addidas first designed great sport shoes, then convinced star athletes to use them. The advertising simply carried through a great sales promotion technique.

American automobiles were designed for identification for years, and the advertising capitalized on fashion changes until unhorsed by changing conditions that made benefits such as lower gas consumption more effective.

Promise advertising can be negative as well as positive. That is, it can promise to eliminate an undesirable condition—"Lose pounds fast," for example.

Identification advertising can also be negative. It is rarely used in product advertising, often in public service advertising: "Don't be stupid! Buckle your seat belt." Negative identification advertising causes the reader, viewer, or listener to become dissociated from the person or quality in the advertisement. It says, "You don't want to be like this, do you?" Note that the dissociation is not based on logic, but on emotion. It is therefore practically impossible to use negative identification in relation to competitors, because it may be slanderous. Even when it's carefully handled to be on the right side of the law, the possibility of backlash limits its use. Anyway, name-callers often bring more opprobrium on themselves than on their antagonists.

There's less danger involved and less skill required in using negative identification in public service advertising, since the injunction in the ad is usually one that everyone agrees is morally correct. After all, who's in favor of forest fires?

If carefully and skillfully used, negative identification can be very effective in product advertising, as can be seen from examples at the end of this chapter.

Neither the identification nor the promise technique is inherently superior. Each has its advantages and disadvantages. It is difficult for a single identification ad to be successful. Repetition is usually necessary so that the imagery will be implanted in prospects' minds. It is also difficult, though not impossible, for identification advertising to be successful in small space. To be in good taste, the advertising can't shout. So small space identification advertising runs the danger of never being noticed.

Advertising with a strong promise can cause a reader to act immediately. And a single ad can be effective. But suppose there's no strong promise that can truthfully be made about the product, service, or company? Sometimes it's the lack of a strong benefit that makes it necessary to rely on identification.

Identification advertising as a whole is admirable, even socially acceptable, because it necessarily appeals to the need to belong to a group. It unifies people. (Every English schoolboy used to learn Henry V's stirring identification speech by heart; Henry Tudor's promise-filled, logical speech is seldom quoted.)

Identification advertising often influences people who say they are not influenced by advertising, yet buy the most advertised products. This kind of advertising does not depend upon a stated benefit, but upon association. It creates an image of the product, service, or company with which the reader, viewer, or listener would like to be associated. Promise advertising may not be admirable, and it is often frowned upon, because it necessarily appeals to the individual's selfish needs and wants. Consequently many advertisers tend to want identification advertising, even though they've never heard the term. They want the kind of advertising they admire and that others admire—such as the most striking cigarette and liquor advertising, for example. They don't want to have the kind of advertising everyone sneers at—advertising that depends upon selfish benefits, that often uses threats: drugs, deodorants, mouthwashes, footpowders, for example. And yet their products may contain the potential for a powerful benefit!

The biggest mistake of this nature, however, is not the use of identification advertising when promise advertising would be more effective. It is the failure to use either. For an ad to be successful it must make the audience *desirous* enough through the promise of a positive benefit, *admiring* enough to identify with the product, service, or company, or *fearful* enough through the use of a direct or implied threat. **Common Mistake #18: Failing to sufficiently arouse the right kind of emotion.**

This mistake can be avoided by realizing that advertising is functional, that advertising must affect people strongly, that innocuous advertising is never effective, and that anything that doesn't relate to a promise or strengthen identification weakens the advertisement. It can be avoided by being realistically aware of the true causes for people doing what they do in this society at this time; and most of all by not being so overwhelmed by the desire to be entertaining, tricky, or contemporary that the basic motivation is smothered or left out.

15

MORE ABOUT
GETTING PEOPLE
TO DO WHAT YOU WANT

Question: I have always been told it is better to be positive than negative. Is this true of advertising?

Answer: Remember the highly successful Moody's headline, "How much could a mistake in investing cost you? $500? $1000? $10,000? More?" This was obviously a negative promise. It was successful because it aroused the emotion of fear. But sometimes the difference between a positive benefit and a negative one is blurred, as one may imply the other. "Do blondes have more fun?" implies that brunettes don't, that coloring your hair will eliminate the dullness from your life. "Wash that gray away" is both positive and negative. "Wash" promises that this will be easier than dyeing. Getting rid of gray, although negative, implies a positive benefit: you'll be as attractive as a younger person.

The difference between positive and negative identification is more critical. We are cautioned early in life against being negative because no one likes a person who threatens, who emphasizes what is bad. Experience shows that the negative promise, skillfully handled, can be the most powerful technique, but improperly handled, it can backfire, and result in disassociation, in negative identification.

Question: "Can the promise and identification techniques be combined?"

Answer: Yes. In fact, it may be that no successful ad ever depends entirely on one or the other. To take an extreme case: the promise of an ugly direct response ad may work better because the style of the ad implies, "Look, this is no baloney. I'm appealing only to your common sense, not to your emotions. You're the kind of guy who is guided by logic, who knows how to save a buck." It appeals to the kind of person who is entranced by the bare pipe-rack environment. Furniture has been very successfully sold on television with this kind of tough-guy-to-tough-guy approach. "If you're a union member . . . you're in" was a key line. Advertising becomes an art when both promise and identification work together to arouse an emotion that brings about the effect desired by the advertiser. The importance of identification makes it essential that copywriters be given information about the audience they're appealing to—and that advertisers establish and remember the nature of their audience when reviewing advertisements.

A TIMELY PROMISE OF A BENEFIT

In 1975, a recession year, most companies followed the usual pattern of reducing their expenditures on capital equipment. Sales of The Bodine Company, a manufacturer of automatic metal-cutting and assembly machines, went down.

However, Bodine makes assembly machines that can cut production costs appreciably. It was felt that if the savings story could be gotten through to top management, and particularly top financial officers of appropriate companies, sales would result.

Previous advertising had concentrated ads in those trade magazines that primarily reach the engineers who initiate the purchase of such machines, and only secondarily aim at top management.

In order to reach the people who make the ultimate decision to buy machines like Bodine's, especially during a recession period, the ad on the following pages was run in *Dunn's Review, Fortune* magazine's Manufacturing Edition, and *Industry Week's* Metalworking Edition.

In the first six weeks after the ad appeared, over two dozen calls were received from Chairmen of the Board, Presidents, and Vice Presidents of companies that were prospective customers.

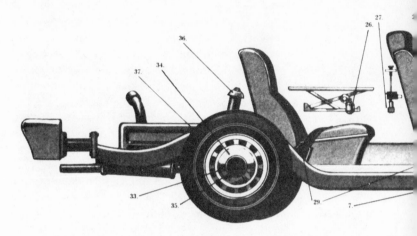

A partial list of small parts and components assembled on Bodine machines for major car manufactur[er]
1. *Thermostats* **2.** *Headlight assemblies* **3.** *Generators* **4.** *Alternators* **5.** *Battery clamps* **6.** *Air conditio[ning]*
valves **7.** *Universal joints* **8.** *Solid-state ignition* **9.** *Voltage regulators* **10.** *Fuel injectors* **11.** *Di[***]*
12. *Carburetors* **13.** *Diverter valves* **14.** *Diaphragm valves* **15.** *Air valves* **16.** *Air pumps* **17.** *Solenoid swit[ches]*
18. *Windshield wipers* **19.** *Armatures* **20.** *Speedometers* **21.** *Cigarette lighters* **22.** *Rearview mirrors* **23.** *[***]*

A Bodine machine
about anything in a ca[r]
And save you up to 95¢ o[n]

Our business at Bodine is making small-parts assembly machines. Not for things like frames and body work — but for assemblies like those listed above.

If you make small parts, we can tell you how to assemble those small parts faster, better — and for far less than it's costing you now.

Think about it for a moment and you'll quickly see why. Industry today is investing literally millions of dollars in trying to cut material and fabricating costs. Trouble is, there's not much room left to cut.

Where the savings are.

The one place left where you can make really significant cost reductions these days is in assembly. That's where your capital expenditures should be, because that's where you stand to save the most. And that's where we can show you how to save up to 95¢ on every assembly dollar.

We know because we've done it for many of America's most successful companies.

Does that mean we can do the same for you? Not necessarily. But 50 years experience in this busi-

ness tells us that 6 of every [***] manufacturers can switch to [***] kind of "selective automation" [***] end up with substantial savings[.]

What kind of savings?

We're not just talking ab[out] labor costs although, obviou[sly] that is a big consideration. You [***] save because your product qua[lity] will improve. Which means y[our] warranty costs will go down. [Fi]nally, you will be able to incre[ase] production substantially without [the] hassle of costly hiring and train[ing] procedures.

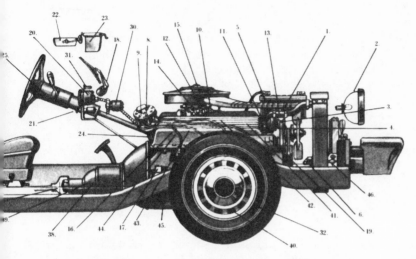

Note the use of an illustration that was likely to attract the attention of the type of reader the advertiser was looking for – suppliers of small parts. Note, too, the straightforward, hard-hitting promise of a benefit in the headline and the clear, easy-to-read, convincing copy, with an ending that tells the reader just what to do. Note, too, the justified use of a double-page spread – primarily necessary for the illustration to be big enough for the reader to pick out the kind of assembly his company produces. The double page was also justified by the large size of the purchase to be made (a very big ticket item), the importance of the subject (cost-cutting in troubled times), and the length of copy necessary for conviction and action-getting.

IDENTIFICATION SELLS CIGARETTES

The introduction of the Virginia Slims 100-millimeter cigarette coincided perfectly with the women's movement – not a moment too soon or too late. TV commercials accented the fact that women no longer needed to stand for the subordinate position they had so long endured, yet the commercials always had a feminine feeling. Handicapped after 1970 by the TV ban on cigarette advertising, Virginia Slims turned to print. From the beginning, advertising of Virginia Slims depended solely upon identification – upon the advertising communicating in an appealing way with words and pictures that this is a cigarette for women who know that times have changed. The copy under the old-fashioned half-tones reads, "In 1914 after 6 years' psychotherapy with the famous Viennese analyst, Frederick Schlinger, Mrs. Ruth Thornbug felt free enough to smoke in his presence. Dr. Schlinger straightened her out." Note that there is absolutely no promise of a benefit in the advertising. Yet wouldn't any woman want to be like the woman in the advertisement? – particularly if she is the independent kind who is going to smoke no matter what authorities say about the health hazard? Full color was used to attract attention and enhance femininity. Note that the rectangular halftones give a feeling of authenticity for the previous condition of women; note the slogan, which is aggressive yet made feminine through the use of "baby"; note the package prominently displayed toward the end of the ad so that it will be remembered when the reader is in a store. Finally, note the lack of earnestness throughout so that no one can be offended. Launched in 1968, Virginia Slims had annual sales of 4.9

In 1914 after 6 years' psychotherapy with the famous Viennese analyst, Frederick Schlinger, Mrs. Ruth Thornburg felt free enough to smoke in his presence.

Dr. Schlinger straightened her out.

You've come a long way, baby.

VIRGINIA SLIMS

Slimmer than the fat cigarettes men smoke.

Fashions: Bieff Herera

Regular: 16 mg."tar," 1.0 mg. nicotine—Menthol: 15 mg."tar," 1.0 mg. nicotine av. per cigarette, FTC Report Oct.'74

billion non-menthol cigarettes and 3.9 billion menthol cigarettes seven years later, outselling several 100's which had been launched earlier and had the advantage of longer TV exposure.

IDENTIFICATION PULLS RECRUITS FOR THE MARINE CORPS

The poster on the opposite page is an excellent example not only of the use of identification but of the use of a poster. Great impact is obtained with few words and a picture. The superiority of the Marines is implied in modern, modest style by the simple, understated words, "a few good men." Three good-looking but realistic men are shown, one black, so that it's easy for a possible recruit to feel that these are the kind of men he'd want to be associated with — to be like. They are shown in the distinctive Marine dress uniform, which again implies superiority. The poster functions well whether the possible recruit is driving past or can stop and write down the telephone number. Note that there is no promise of a benefit such as learning a trade or good pay or a pension. Just identification. The Marine Corps has the smallest advertising budget of any of the other three services, but this slogan ranked higher in recognition by enlistees than any of the other service slogans. Despite intense competition from the other services resulting from the all-volunteer force and the higher standards, the Marine Corps continued to attract more men than it had places for. The agency was J. Walter Thompson.

NEGATIVE IDENTIFICATION PULLS TELEPHONE CALLS

The recruiting advertisement on page 72 is a rare example of negative identification. This ad was used by a major brokerage firm to help staff a new uptown office in New York City. Most brokerage offices are downtown in the Wall Street area. This meant that many registered representatives who commuted from the suburbs were forced to ride a crowded, dirty subway after and before a long train trip. The telephone rang practically continuously throughout the day this two-column advertisement appeared in *The New York Times*, and numerous mail inquiries were received. A high percentage were of appropriate caliber; in fact, this advertisement was the biggest single source of personnel for the office. Note how the copy swings immedi-

Is this how a registered representative with an income of $30,000 a year should start his day?

Shouldn't he travel in dignity? Shouldn't he, in fact, be pampered by the investment firm he works for? Have a private office. Handsomely furnished. With a pleasant view. In a modern, attractive building.

Shouldn't he be freed from noise and every possible irritation? Be supplied with top-notch secretarial and clerical assistance.

If you're a broker with substantial production, this may be your chance to live your day in the style you wish. One of the country's most highly regarded securities underwriters is expanding its brokerage facilities—is opening an office uptown, a few steps from Grand Central. Your personal office will look out over Park Avenue. It will be in a brand-new building. Your associates will have achieved the same kind of success you have.

You will join this firm mostly as a matter of personal pride. In representing this particular firm. In the physical surroundings in which you will work. In the quality of your associates.

You may make more money as well. By having a suitable environment in which to meet your clients. And by being able to offer them numerous new issues, secondaries and over-the-counter blocks.

For more information, telephone WHitehall 4-0676 today between 10:00 a.m. and 5:00 p.m. This is a direct, private line to the vice president with overall responsibility for the new uptown office. If telephoning is inconvenient, write Vice President, Box ——, New York Times. All letters will be promptly acknowledged.

Telephone or write today, even if you would prefer to defer joining this firm until after January 1, 1968. A good man is worth waiting for.

ately into positive identification, how the validity of the copy is enhanced by eliminating all that can be degrading about getting a new job: The telephone number to call is "a direct, private line to the vice president . . ." The copy does promise a benefit—"You may make more money as well"—but the benefit is subordinate to the identification. The square news-style photo adds to the conviction. Incidentally, it was a stock photograph so the cost of production was low. The agency was Benn & MacDonough, Inc.

TELEPHONE COMPANY TV COMMERCIAL

(For the entire 30 seconds the camera holds steadily on two telephone booths, side by side. In one is a dark-haired man, in the other a light-haired man. Both are in their late twenties or early thirties.)

In Booth One

(Dark-haired man is looking up number in telephone book.)

DARK-HAIRED MAN: (to himself) Shoemaker—Shoemaker. Margie Shoemaker. Jefferson Street . . .
(He finds number, begins dialing.)
Hello, Margie? Big Bob here. The fellow from the party, uh, in the brown sweater. (pause) (laughs) Yeah, I know, how could you forget? Hey, listen, uh, how you doing. . . .

In Booth Two

LIGHT-HAIRED MAN: (on the phone holding a hand-scribbled note in his hand) Hello, operator, I'm looking for the number of Margie Shoemaker. (pause)
I don't know, it could be a *u* or an *o*. (pause)
On Jackson Street. (pause)
Oh, I'm sorry that's Jefferson Street. (pause)
What was that? 555-2362.
Thank you very much. (to himself) 555-2362.
(dials)
(busy signal)

Superimposed:

Look it up yourself. It's faster. C & P Telephone

The purpose of the commercial shown on the preceding page was to cause people to look up telephone numbers themselves rather than asking for directory assistance. The exact budget is confidential but more than $101,000 and less than $500,000 was expended for support of an internal company effort. Total savings to the telephone company from the full program were estimated at $5,750,000 for the year. Calculations were based on the actual reduction in calls to operators for directory assistance and the additional wages and equipment that would have been necessary for the calls not made.

Note that the power of this Ketchum, MacLeod & Grove commercial derives from visual demonstration—and an unusual combination of all four ways of convincing people. Superficially the commercial utilizes a positive benefit—"Look it up yourself. It's faster"—contrasted with a negative promise of wasting time. But actually a direct hard sell along this line couldn't compete against the trouble of looking up the number. The true power of the commercial derives from identification positive and negative. The viewer wants to be like the guy who gets the girl, not like the fumbling fool who fails. And the inoffensive sexual humor makes the point of the commercial memorable. Yet note how simple and direct it is.

WHICH HELP-WANTED AD PULLED BETTER IN EACH CASE?

Three pairs of employment advertisements appear below. To the uninitiated eye, there is little difference between those in each pair, yet one ad in each case pulled more than twice as many as its mate. Each pair appeared in the same newspaper on the same day.

Version A

SECRETARY, exciting opportunity for you with top firm. Varied duties. Park free, benefits, $548
Toni Star 585-5841   312 S. 4th
Snelling & Snelling Personnel

Version B

SECRETARY—Advertising
Exciting, rewarding job. Big opportunity to get into copy writing. Lots of fringes. $550. Fee paid to right girl. Hurry.
Phone Jim Best   585-5848
Snelling & Snelling Personnel

Version A

Leading National Tire Company requires
WAREHOUSE MANAGER
No experience necessary but would be an asset. Excellent medical fringe benefits. Apply Box 349 Leader-Post

Version B

Are you capable of managing our warehouse?
IF SO—
Our tire company needs you. Experience an asset. Reply Box 362, Leader-Post

Version A

AIDE/SECY. $8500
Young Lawyer
Will Train
$8500 Fee Paid
This young attorney is only age 29, but already has an excellent reputation. He is involved in the current energy crisis—he is dedicated to his work and needs someone to help as his secretary. No experience necessary, if you can type well and want to learn about law and all its interesting facets. Call 659-5791 for appt.
ALBERS PERSONNEL, 1700 K st., n.w. (agency)

Version B

SECY./AIDE   FEE PAID
$8500
Your First Step In
Secretarial World
NO EXPERIENCE
NECESSARY
If you can type and want to learn about law and all its interesting facts, let me introduce you to this young attorney who needs your help and willing to train you. Call Ms. Wilson
659-5791
or come in today, ALBERS PERSONNEL, 1701 K St. N.W. (Agency)

HOW HELP WANTED ADS COMPARED

In the first pair, Version A pulled 1 reply, Version B pulled 7. In the second pair, Version A pulled 30 replies, Version B pulled 14. In the third pair, Version A pulled 14 replies, Version B 7. In each instance, the winning ad promised more and made the job sound more like the one the reader would like to identify with.*

Version B of the first ad for a secretary promises "a rewarding job. Big opportunity to get into copywriting. Lots of fringes . . . Fee paid." Its competitor offers only "Park free, benefits." B pulled seven replies, A only one.

The A Version of the tire company ad promises "Excellent medical fringe benefits." It makes the job sound better by using a title the reader would like to have — Warehouse Manager — instead of merely describing the work he must do — managing a warehouse. It increases identification by informing the reader that the company is one he would be proud to work for, a "Leading National Tire Company," instead of a company nobody ever heard of. With fourteen replies, Version B did not do badly; but Version A pulled thirty replies.

Identification alone made ad A for the legal secretary outpull ad B by fourteen replies to seven. Version B makes the job sound dull and psychologically unrewarding. Version A makes the same job seem exciting. The respondent would be a team-mate, helping to tackle one of the world's most critical problems, the energy crisis.

* The selected advertisements are from a study made by the Newspaper Advertising Bureau. The study made helpful comments but did not say this.

16

A NEW AND COMPLETE THEORY OF COPYWRITING

Here are five sound copy principles:

1. Put a benefit in the headline.
2. Use short, concrete, familiar words.
3. Put the brand name in the headline.
4. What you say is more important than how you say it.
5. Put a time limit on the offer.

All of these principles have been tested by time. They have helped thousands of copywriters create an untold number of successful advertisements. They have helped many an executive guide and judge copy.

But each has a serious defect—a defect contained in every rule of copywriting. No rule is valid in every set of circumstances.

The Virginia Slims advertising not only doesn't have a benefit in the headline—there's none even in the copy.

Short, concrete, familiar words make for easy reading, but in some advertising—for perfume, for example—emotional tone is more important than easy reading. Strange words, even coined words, can give a unique feeling, the way French words on a menu make the food more intriguing and worth the additional cost.

Putting the brand name in the headline of a package advertisement ties the name closely to the promise or identification, but plenty of package goods advertisements—Preparation H ads, for example—

have been very effective without following this rule. And it certainly doesn't apply to direct response or image advertising.

What an advertisement says — what it offers, its content — places an upper limit on the effectiveness of the advertisement, a fact too often forgotten. But suppose what is being offered is trivial — such as the choice between two different kinds of detergent. And the triviality must be remembered for days, until the viewer, reader, or listener goes to the supermarket. Then the *form* of the advertising — the technique used to make the triviality seem consequential and make it memorable — becomes more important than the content.

Putting a time limit on an offer in direct response advertising almost always increases responses. But it can also be self-defeating when the approach is soft sell. The humorous commercial for Lanier dictating equipment would obviously have been less effective if listeners had been urged to "Act now!"

The general lack of understanding of the limitations of these and other principles of copywriting has always had important, disastrous consequences.

A copywriter with a string of successes in one type of advertising — say image — fails miserably in another type — say package goods.

An advertiser hears about a certain principle and insists on it for his advertising when it doesn't apply.

Copy supervisors kill copy that would be effective.

Account executives find it impossible to convince copywriters that their copy is inappropriate, and vice versa.

And an advertising agency that has done wonders with one kind of account, such as automobiles, fails miserably on a different kind of account, such as cigarettes.

Common Mistake #19: Applying a sound copy principle at the wrong time.

The paragraphs that follow make it possible for the first time for copywriters and executives to see when the principles they have been successfully following continue to apply and when they don't. This chapter now makes intelligent communication about copy possible between advertising people with different backgrounds, skills, and experiences.

The limitations and applicability of every copy principle are determined by six conditions.

One condition is the *purpose* of the advertising. In direct response advertising (the Moody's ad, for example), the *purpose* is to cause the audiences to act immediately in a certain way—telephone, write, or visit. In package goods advertising, the *purpose* is to cause the audience to remember the brand and choose it in the days that follow. (See the L'eggs commercial at the end of this chapter.) In corporate image advertising (the ITT ad, for example), the *purpose* is to cause the audience to feel that the company is their kind of company.

The *purpose* most directly affects the ending of the advertisement or commercial. If the *purpose* is to cause the reader to respond immediately, the ending motivates him or her to do so. The exact technique may vary, depending upon the other conditions, but the principal possibilities are: including a coupon, urging the reader to act, putting a time limit on the offer, repeating the telephone number, or choosing a telephone number or box number that's easy to remember. (See the Moody's and Bodine ads.)

However, if the *purpose* of the advertising is to cause people to ask for the brand in a store, then the brand name obviously should be big and prominent in a print ad or repeated often in a commercial. (As in the Parker Pen ad and the L'eggs commercial.)

If the *purpose* of the advertising is also or primarily to cause people to select the brand from a shelf, then it's intelligent to prominently display the package in the advertising, as in the L'eggs, Mitchum, and Diaparene Baby Wash Cloths commercials at the end of this chapter.

Since the *purpose* of a corporate identity advertisement is to cause the company's name to be remembered, a successful ad of this type usually ends with the company name, prominently displayed. (As in the ITT print ad.) However, it may be counterproductive to directly and specifically urge the reader, viewer, or listener to remember the name. It may destroy the impression of, say, dignity, solidity, and character that the advertisement is attempting to convey. It is usually preferable to make the name memorable without seeming overmuch to attempt to do so.

Clarity is naturally essential in all advertising copy, but if the *purpose* is to get action immediately, any lack of clarity whatsoever is fatal. A well-written direct response advertisement moves the reader from interest aroused by the headline, to a desire for the product, to actual physical movement. Any confusion in meaning usually results in the reader's turning the page and being lost forever.

This means the use of short, familiar, concrete words. Sentences, if not short, must be carefully constructed so there's never any need for rereading. Abstract words and flowery adjectives are to be eschewed.

This is not always a valid principle when the *purpose* of the advertising is to leave the audience with a certain feeling toward the product, service, or company. Adjectives can be emotionally loaded and sentences can be long, although they should be carefully constructed. If the reader fails to understand a word or a sentence, or even stops reading after a paragraph or sooner, the advertisement doesn't necessarily fail. The illustration and headline usually do most of the work in this kind of advertising anyway.

The *purpose* of the advertising also affects the beginning. However, the beginning is also strongly affected by another condition: The *attitude of the audience.*

Sometimes the *audience* takes an active interest in the advertising. Their *attitude* is, "Where can I buy window glass?" or some other specific item, as when they pick up the Yellow Pages. Or they want to know what's being offered, as when they turn to help-wanted advertising. More often, the *audience* is uninterested. They want to read the articles in the newspaper or continue to watch the television program. The advertisement must then begin with words or illustrations that will attract many readers' attention away from the editorial matter.

A typical classified advertisement, on the other hand, need not begin the same way. Classified advertisements of houses for sale usually and correctly begin with the area in which the house is located and the price—with facts which tell the reader whether he should continue reading that particular ad or not. The help-wanted ads at the end of the previous chapter correctly begin with the job title.

Successful corporate identity advertisements begin with illustrations and headlines that have a broad appeal—that will interest a large number of readers.

The most consistently effective opening for a corporate identity advertisement has proved to be a dominant human-interest photograph, but other techniques have been effective as well. There are few limitations to the copywriter's creativity because of the broad nature of the *purpose*, which is usually to cause the company to be favorably remembered. The ITT ad is a successful example.

The beginning of a package goods advertisement, on the other hand, must direct itself to people who need the product or service currently.

Every headline and illustration is selective. None attracts every reader. Only very large, very effective advertisements attract the attention of over half of the readers of a publication. Entertaining beginnings attract people looking for entertainment. A picture of a dog attracts the attention of people who like dogs.

The requirements of a typical direct response advertisement are the most rigid of all. It is not enough just to attract the reader's attention. Experience has proved that headlines and illustrations that are merely startling – arouse curiosity only – usually result in few responses.

A typical direct response advertisement has as its *purpose* immediate action, yet it must deal with a disinterested, even hostile *audience attitude*. With a few words and perhaps an illustration – and within minutes – it must cause the reader to take an action he hadn't been contemplating. It's a tremendous task.

The beginnings of direct response advertisements must therefore not only attract a good number of readers, but also select the kind of readers most likely to clip the coupon or make the telephone call and motivate them to read the copy eagerly. A strong benefit will do this.

A corporate identity advertisement may successfully depend solely upon curiosity. A package goods advertisement may depend upon curiosity plus a marginal benefit or positive identification. But it is difficult to cause a significant number of readers to act immediately through positive identification or a trivial promise.

Note that in direct response advertising the name of the brand need not be – in fact usually should not be – in the headline. What the reader buys is the benefit or benefits. He must be moved to act, not to choose. The name of the brand or of the company is incidental, unless it is already known to the reader and enhances the credibility of the promise.

The attitude of the reader affects the length of copy in a print advertisement, and determines whether a 30-second commercial or a long-length commercial should be used.

In advertising that asks the *audience* to send money, long copy is necessary if the advertisement is to pull well. The copy has much to do. It must interest the reader, then convince him that it would be worth his time, effort, and money to tear out the coupon, fill it out, get out his checkbook, write a check, find a stamp and an envelope, write the address, and mail it. His emotions must be aroused and directed, and any reasons he may have for not acting must be overcome.

In package goods advertising short copy is usually appropriate, because the *attitude of the audience* is that the subject is trivial. It would be impossible to hold the reader's attention through long copy. However, if what is being discussed is important, long copy can on occasion be successfully used as in the ads for Vantage cigarettes.

A third condition that affects the beginning of the advertisement or commercial — as well as other aspects — is the *medium* in which it appears: newspaper, magazine, radio, television, outdoor, or transit.

A writer for radio or television has more freedom than a print copywriter. The headline and/or illustration of a print advertisement must *attract* attention; the beginning of a radio or TV commercial need only *hold* attention, because the audience is already listening or watching. This means, for example, that a direct response commercial can (but need not) lead into the benefit more gently, even indirectly, than is necessary in a print advertisement.

In addition to the effect on the opening, the *medium* affects the degree of conciseness.

Suppose, for example, an advertiser gets some free radio time. He has a print advertisement with copy that lasts about a minute. It sounds smooth when read aloud, so he uses it for his radio commercial.

What's wrong with that?

Just this: If it's a well-written print advertisement, it's probably a poor radio commercial. A good writer modifies the way he writes to take full advantage of the medium. One of the advantages of print is that it can be read at the reader's own pace, and can be reread. Consequently, as compared to a radio commercial, the meaning in a print advertisement can be concise, even compressed. More information can be communicated with fewer words.

Consequently a well-written print advertisement read aloud will attempt to communicate too much in too few words. Consider the brand name or the name of the advertiser. If either is in big print in the ad, it need not be repeated. Whereas in a radio commercial, the name must be repeated again and again if the listener is to remember it. In radio, this is an advantage. In a print ad, if the name is repeated again and again, the reader is likely to turn the page. But radio and television are continuous media; the listener must stay tuned if he wants to hear the rest of the program.

The need for repetition in spoken communication is suggested by the use of the double negative and the repeated negative. Shakespeare used the double negative on occasion (a fact glossed over by most English teachers) because he wrote for the ear, not for the printed page. Standard military practice over the radio is to repeat the negative, to say "... not, I say again, *not* ..." so that there can be no misunderstanding.

In a direct response commercial, it is of course most important that the telephone number or the address be repeated.

The *medium* also affects sentence structure. A radio announcer can smoothly emphasize any word or phrase in a sentence. In print copy italics, boldface, and underlining can be used for emphasis, but must be used sparingly or the effect is jarring and distasteful. Skillful print writers are therefore careful to put key words where they are most conspicuous: at the ends and beginnings of sentences. This is not necessary in radio and television writing.

The *medium* affects the choice of words. A skillful print writer chooses words not only for their meaning but for the attitude and emotion they convey. He sometimes uses words which, while not entirely unknown, may yet be a little strange to most readers. On radio, the listener may be baffled by an unfamiliar word when he hears it just once in passing. Furthermore, using words for their emotional quality is not as important in spoken language. The tone of the speaker's voice can convey attitude and emotion much more powerfully than the most carefully chosen word in print.

The length of time the audience can take to comprehend the message has an overriding importance. That's why ten-second commercials and roadside billboards have much in common. It's difficult to use either for image advertising. All that can generally be done is to direct the buyer's attention to the advertiser's brand or to the company itself. "Last gasoline stop for 100 miles" is an example. But note the modifier "roadside." Billboards in subway and train stations and car cards in subways and buses can have more words because the reader has more time. It is the time allowed the audience by the physical form of the *medium* that makes it necessary for roadside billboards and ten-second commercials to restrict themselves almost entirely to identifying the advertiser in a favorable way.

The *medium* is sometimes important enough to affect the entire advertising concept. Certain forms – slogans, jingles, slice-of-life and other dramatizations – are much more effective on radio and television than in print.

Television is a more powerful persuader than print or radio because the viewer receives the message through two of his senses at the same time. However, what the television viewer *sees* affects him more strongly than what he *hears*. It is a worse tragedy to be blind than deaf.

Yet all too often a television commercial will consist of a studio announcer reading copy with all the necessary information carried in the sound rather than in the picture.

This sometimes occurs because the production cost is lower, but more often for a more insidious reason. Often the advertiser is shown a script or at best a story-board for approval, because the words carry more impact in this form. It's difficult for the advertiser to visualize how the movement of the actors, the intonations they give the words, the lighting, the cutting, and all the other paraphernalia of show business will affect the impact of the commercial. Consequently it's safer for the agency to present commercials with the sound carrying the burden of the message rather than the picture.

Common Mistake #20: Failing to fully utilize the peculiar advantages of the medium, especially television.

The telephone-booth commercial that follows the previous chapter, for example, does not seem very powerful on the printed page. It could only be effective on television. Television allows the viewer to follow the words and action in both telephone booths simultaneously. The man who asks for the number can be directly compared with the man who looks up the number and gets the girl first.

A fourth condition that determines the way an advertisement or commercial must be written to succeed is the *nature of the audience*. An older audience is more tradition-minded, more conservative. Incomplete sentences, incorrect grammar of any kind, or vulgarity may cause them to want to disassociate themselves from the advertiser. Savings institutions, for example, have found that modern-looking advertisements don't draw as many sizable deposits as old-fashioned ads do, because the older people have the money.

Cola commercials, on the other hand, try to appeal to the biggest users of their product – young people. Therefore the video portion shows teen-agers, the audio portion features their kind of music, and the lyrics echo their philosophy.

Consider socioeconomic class. People at higher income levels seem to have better taste. Or at least they seem to want to associate themselves with what is tasteful. It's no coincidence that commercials for investment houses, banks, and similar institutions do well on New York's radio station WQXR, which features classical music. Vulgarity can be counterproductive in advertising to a high socioeconomic class.

On the other hand, advertisements that feature the hearty, strong, masculine, vigorous qualities of the blue collar class—beer commercials, for example—can increase sales to a high-school-educated, middle-income audience.

So far the conditions have ignored one immutable determinant of the copy: *what is being advertised.*

All too often discussions of advertising pay scant attention to the fact that some products and services are easier to advertise successfully than others.

Regulations of the Securities and Exchange Commission and the New York Stock Exchange inhibit investment advertising, for example. Regulations of the Federal Trade Commission make prescription drug advertising difficult. Some products such as automobiles, clothing, and food are attractive by their very nature. They have inherent consumer benefits. In ads for items like these, it generally makes sense to feature a dominant, realistic photograph of the product. The reader sees the consumer benefit at once, and the copy can then deal with brand differences.

Other products, however, such as those sold for industrial use, may reveal their consumer benefits only when shown in action. Yet some office equipment people just show the machines they make. What could be duller?

It is difficult for an advertiser to objectively judge whether his product has inherent appeal. He may be inclined to believe it has appeal because it's his product. He may have gone into the transistor business because the whole idea of controlling electrical flow with miniature elements fascinated him. It doesn't necessarily fascinate the people he is trying to sell, however. They're more interested in their own products. They want to know how his transistors will make the radios they assemble, for example, function better or cost less to produce.

More often, advertisers go to the other extreme. Their product or service seems boring to them because they've been working with it for so long. They feel that their advertising must do something extraordinary, perhaps even show a naked girl, in order to get attention.

In short, **Common Mistake #21: Failing to capitalize on the inherent nature of the product, service, or company.**

This is where the advertising agency should star. Not only is the agency objective, but its people may have independent proof of the relative appeals of different kinds of products. If they're conscientious, they've studied the results of the testing of hundreds of advertisements, as described in a later chapter. These tests clearly show for which products it is easy to get high readership, for which it is terribly difficult, and which are in-between. The agency may know, for example, when it helps to show people in an advertisement — which is most of the time — and when it detracts. In food advertising, for example, showing people eating generally cuts readership. Seeing someone else eating is not attractive.

Some products are intangible — services like education, stock brokerage, and banking, for instance. Some are both intangible and inherently unattractive — such as life insurance and funeral services. In these industries, the copywriter faces the greatest challenge. How can attention be gained? How can the benefit be explained, or shown, or implied? No matter how brilliant the copywriter, it is unlikely that his efforts for services of this kind will ever win important advertising awards.

Whether a product is tangible or intangible makes a difference in the kind of words that are most effective. If it is intangible, the advertising is usually more effective when the words are concrete and the sentences short and easy to follow. The task, after all, is to make the abstract perceptible. If the product is tangible, the task of the copy may be to give it a certain aura — that is, give it meaning beyond itself, as in perfume or wine advertising. The words therefore may be abstract, flowery, and emotional, and the sentences longer and more involved.

The sixth and final condition sometimes makes an enormous difference in the copy strategy, sometimes it is of no importance at all. It is the *competition.*

If two brands are more or less equal, featuring a marginal difference for one brand in a direct response advertisement will not produce increased sales. In fact, the advertising will probably fail. A direct response advertisement must promise a benefit strong enough to grab the reader and make him act immediately. What counts is whether the advertisement makes him feel that by sending for the product right away, he will benefit strongly. The *competition* isn't there to compete.

In package goods advertising, the *competition* is usually all-important. The consumer must choose between two brands of soap, sitting side by side on the supermarket shelf. If the advertiser's brand is significantly superior, advertising its superiority clearly, strongly, and memorably can make consumers choose that brand. If the advertiser's brand has a marginal difference, the advertising can be effective by dramatizing this marginal difference, causing the buyer to choose the marginally superior brand. If there's no advertisable marginal difference – or if identification will be more effective – then identification can be used.

The *competition* is especially important when a company is not the leader in its industry.

Studies have shown that companies that are not number one often increase the sales of the leading brand with their advertising. Although no one knows for certain why this happens, there are a couple of theories: (1) The TV viewer is stimulated by the commercial to buy the *product* but not the *brand*, and since the leader's name is more familiar he or she buys the leading brand. (2) The viewer remembers the benefit promised by the non-leader, but forgets that brand, so the benefit is associated with the leader.

It is obviously more important, therefore, for the non-leader to emphasize an advantage offered by his brand than it is for the leader to stress brand advantage. If the leader has 50 percent or more of the market, it may be in his interest to use his advertising primarily to stimulate product usage, thus increasing overall sales.

Yet many a non-leader in a highly competitive industry has advertising that thoughtlessly imitates the leader in the industry. It derives from a feeling of inferiority by companies that are not number one in sales. Their managements feel that the leader must know more than they do, that's why he's the leader, so they just imitate the leader's copy platform and media strategy. Then they won't be criticized.

Common Mistake #22: Promoting the sale of a competitor's brand. It can be avoided by adopting one of the strategies advertising people group under the word "positioning."

One positioning strategy works like this: The advertiser picks a *segment* of the market to appeal to. He doesn't try to appeal to the entire market. That's what the leader must generally do — and that's the leader's handicap.

The non-leader concentrates his advertising on some of that audience and makes them feel his product or service or company is right for them. He may even be able to select the most profitable segment of the market and concentrate on it.

That's what Schaefer beer did. Their marketing people asked themselves, "What's the most profitable segment of the beer drinking audience?" The answer was so easy it was laughable: "Those who drink the most beer." So a slogan was fashioned — "when you're having more than one" — and appropriate commercials and advertisements were written and produced. Over a period of years this strategy moved Schaefer up from number three in sales in the New York Metropolitan area to number one.

For the non-leaders to successfully compete with Schaefer, they then had to appeal to the less profitable segments of the market.

Note that Schaefer used the copy technique of identification. The viewer was made to feel that the product was especially suited to him. But positioning may also involve media selection. Beer drinkers are necessarily a mass audience — whether they are heavy drinkers or not — so Schaefer had to use the same principal medium as its competitors, television.

However, a positioning strategy that called for appealing, say, to those seeking quality and willing to pay a higher price might call for advertising in upper-income magazines when the leader was on TV or in newspapers.

When positioning depends solely upon identification, as in the instances of Schaefer and Virginia Slims, many millions of dollars are necessary for success. But if there is a real and powerful benefit for a segment of the audience, positioning can succeed with very much less money, perhaps a few thousand dollars. The Tylenol ad elsewhere in the book is a case in point.

The most common positioning strategy is to accent a marginal difference. Suppose, for example, that an image survey were taken in a service business, and users ranked the leader, a non-leader, and most other companies in the business as follows on the three characteristics indicated. Ten is the maximum score.

	Leader	Non-leader	Average for several other companies
Full Range of Services	9	9	8.8
Individual Attention	8	7	7.2
A Third Quality	6	6	5.0

Suppose further that the leader is stressing a full range of services and individual attention in his advertising. This may be the best strategy for him. It is hardly likely, however, that it is also the best strategy for the non-leader. He can best improve his image, both in relation to what it is now and in relation to the leader, by stressing a third quality. What's more, he will attract people who don't realize that this third quality is offered by the leader as well. (See the Diaparene Baby Wash Cloth commercial that follows.)

The marginal quality stressed by the campaign for Avis Rent A Car was "We try harder." The copy appeared to emphasize benefits, clean ashtrays, for example, but it is likely that the desire to identify with a company that had an admirable attitude was a greater factor.

Sometimes even an apparent drawback can be turned to advantage. Early Volkswagen ads stressed the car's unusual ugliness. This appealed to that segment of the car-buying market that was turned off by Detroit's slickness.

Sometimes relating to the leader is more important than how the relating is done. It may be that the #2 position so starkly stated in the Avis advertising is what counted most. The highly successful Seven-Up advertising, with its Uncola theme, does little more than note that Seven-Up is an alternative to a cola drink. Honeywell is apparently doing well in computers with its "The Other Computer Company" advertising. The point is this: in a competitive industry, when the function of the advertising is to cause prospective users to choose, the competition cannot be ignored. What is more, a brand's competitive position can be turned to its own advantage.

To recap the six conditions that determine the most effective ways to write and illustrate an ad or commercial:

Purpose—that is, what the advertising is expected to accomplish.

Attitude of the audience—the degree of existing interest or lack of interest.

Medium—the physical way the message is communicated.

Nature of the audience—interests, ability to buy, customs, prejudices, knowledge, intelligence, and so on.

What is being advertised—the qualities of the product, service, or company.

Competition—how the product, service, or company compares with others in sales and advertising volume.

Any influence can be categorized under one of these six conditions. They are not theoretical. These conditions actually exist. They derive from the function of advertising: to communicate information about *what is being advertised* to an *audience* through a *medium* so that a specific *purpose* is accomplished. For easier understanding, the *audience* has been considered under three headings: *attitude of the audience*, *nature of the audience*, and how the audience relates the product, service, or company to the leader—*competition*.

Judgment must still be exercised by executives. Ingenuity is still necessary for copywriters and art directors. Copywriting will always be an art because of the variety of human beings and their interests —and because today's bright idea becomes tomorrow's cliché. These conditions, however, make it possible for a copywriter's ingenuity to be effectively directed. A copywriter who keeps them in mind is not likely to create a startlingly original ad that won't do the advertiser much good. What's more, he will be better able to convince others that an ad he believes to be great really is great.

This list of conditions makes it possible for executives to quickly and efficiently judge copy. It gives them a rational basis for accepting or rejecting an advertisement. And makes it possible for them to vocalize sound reasons for rejections or requested modifications. Their comments are likely to result in the next version being superior rather than just different.

These conditions make it possible for anyone—advertiser, art director, review board, account executive, even the spouse of the advertiser—to make intelligent, constructive comments about advertising copy and art.

MORE ABOUT THOSE VOLKSWAGEN ADS

It is now easier to see why the Volkswagen advertisements following Chapter 12 were so successful. The *purpose* of the advertising was to motivate readers to visit dealer showrooms, so the copy is full of promises. At the same time, the style of both layout and copy encourages identification among people who believe they are guided by reason, and who not only don't want a status based on conspicuous consumption but enjoy being a little different. The *attitude of the audience* is interest in the editorial content of the magazine, so an illustration is chosen that will attract the attention of those most likely to act on the proposition being offered. People who are in the market for an automobile are attracted by a picture of an automobile. The original medium was magazines so photographs reproduced well and concise copy was appropriate.

The great genius of the Volkswagen ad creators, however, was in their exploitation of the inherent qualities of the product — of *what is being advertised* — and of the *competition*.

There were two classes of competitors: American cars and foreign cars. American car advertising was fashion-oriented. Drawings were often used to make the cars appear big, beautiful, and sleek. Foreign cars at that time had a bad name, because the lower-priced makes had not performed as well as their buyers had anticipated. Volkswagen challenged both competitors by featuring The Beetle as functional and reliable — which it was — and by doing so in a believable way.

The believability was enhanced in two ways. First, by the straightforward layout. And second, by accenting instead of trying to disguise the car's obvious drawback — its appearance. One headline read: "Ugly is only skin deep." Another ad showed a two-car garage at night with only a Volkswagen in it. The headline: "It does all the work but on Saturday night who goes to the party?" Note that the humor makes fun of the product, not the buyer.

Many of the ads had benefit headlines. "The only water a Volkswagen needs is the water you wash it with." "It won't drive you to the poorhouse." "One of the nice things about owning it is selling it." The more humorous ads increased the readership of the benefit headline ads, and the more self-deprecating ones increased credibility. It was the campaign that was successful; it was impossible to tell which individual ads were most effective.

A DISCIPLINED APPROACH TO MARKETING AND ADVERTISING ACHIEVES A MARKETING BREAKTHROUGH

Hanes Corporation had developed a new, different, and superior hosiery product — a super-stretch panty hose that had no shape until

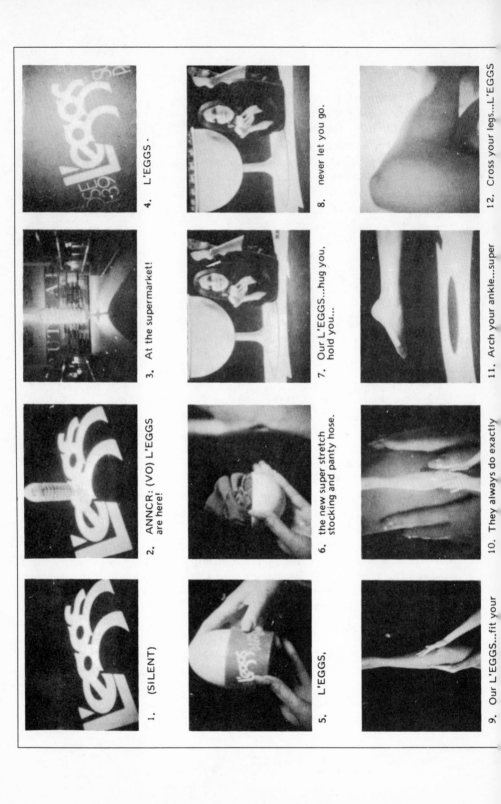

1. (SILENT)

2. ANNCR: (VO) L'EGGS are here!

3. At the supermarket!

4. L'EGGS -

5. L'EGGS,

6. the new super stretch stocking and panty hose.

7. Our L'EGGS....hug you, hold you...

8. never let you go.

9. Our L'EGGS...fit your

10. They always do exactly

11. Arch your ankle....super

12. Cross your legs...L'EGGS

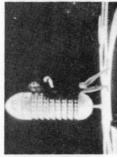

13. Bend...super-stretch L'EGGS hold...along the back.

14. Straighten out...no bagging at the knee.

15. Our L'EGGS super-stretch out and super-stretch back.

16. Our L'EGGS super-stretch to do...exactly what your legs are doing.

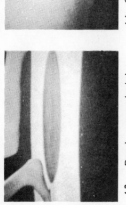
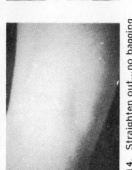

17. Get a new pair of L'EGGS ...at your supermarket boutique.

18. 89¢ for stockings... $1.39 for panty hose.

19. Anyway you stretch your legs, we stretch our L'EGGS

20. too.

the woman pulled it on. It then shaped itself to conform to her leg. The product not only won out over every other product tested against it, but the single size reduced the inventory a retailer needed to maintain.

In 1969, Hanes had research conducted to ascertain the possibility of marketing the new product, not in the traditional way, but through supermarkets and drugstores. These are the outlets where a housewife shops most often, and where she buys most of her branded items. The research showed that a substantial market already existed in food outlets, that there were 600 different brands, that none enjoyed more than a four-percent share of the market, that hosiery then being sold through supermarkets and drugstores had a low quality image, and that advertising or promotion was usually based on price alone.

It was decided that a marketing opportunity existed, and that a properly-designed, complete, and integrated marketing program could make the new brand a planned purchase. It was necessary to create a name, a package, and a display for the new product that would separate it immediately from the multitude of hosiery brands already in existence. Ideally name, package, and display would be integrated, so that when a consumer thought of one she thought of the other. Hence "L'eggs," descriptive of the package and the use of the product, also feminine, contemporary, and memorable. The pun was chosen not for humor or shock effect, although these were a plus, but because the double meaning functionally described both the package and its contents.

Ten million dollars was spent on national advertising in virtually all media: day and evening television, magazines, Sunday supplements, and local newspapers. This was *double* the amount spent by the entire hosiery industry for manufacturer's brands in the previous year.

The *purpose* of the Dancer Fitzgerald Sample advertising was to make women want the brand, to associate the brand with a supermarket or drugstore (a supermarket especially), and to remember the brand when they next visited one of those outlets.

The introductory commercial on the preceding pages shows how women were made to want L'eggs – by promising a good fit under all conditions (both positive and negative benefits are used). The association with a supermarket is made directly by showing the display in a supermarket both at the beginning and end of the commercial. The memorability is enhanced by showing the name big at the beginning, and by repeating it twelve times in the audio.

The *attitude of the television audience* is that they want entertainment, but they'll give what comes next on the screen a chance, so their attention is held by the curiosity appeal of the unusual name and the announcement of something new. (The print ads began with promise of the benefit, partly because the reader has to be attracted away from the editorial and therefore must be given stronger initial motivation. One print ad had the illustration of a girl's legs upside down on a swing. The headline was: "L'eggs hug me, hold me, never let me go . . .").

The commercial takes full advantage of the *medium*. The benefit is demonstrated visually and emphasized in the audio. A viewer could understand the commercial only by looking or only by listening, yet both the audio and video complement each other, increasing the commercial's power exponentially.

The *nature of the audience* is practically every woman, so different types were used in each commercial. Some showed several different types in the same commercial. The language has connotations of beauty and love. Can you imagine using "hug you" in a commercial aimed at men? Note how the commercial appeals to the self-interest of women, their need to be attractive: "you" or "yours" is used ten times in that one minute.

What is being advertised is a product of continual interest to women. Therefore, introducing the product itself early—as in the case of automobiles for men—increases attention. L'eggs are low-cost and therefore likely to be tried once if the benefits sound good. It is not as important to make a strong case for quality or reliability for a low-cost item as it is for a high-cost item.

The *competition* consists of the 600 or more other brands being sold through supermarkets and drugstores. The brand must therefore be shown to be superior, yet a good buy (89¢ for stockings and $1.39 for pantyhose are low prices).

The L'eggs program was an immediate success. In six months over 40% of all women had tried L'eggs at least once. Testing of the commercials showed that recall of their message was far above average. Thus L'eggs became the best-selling hosiery brand in the United States.

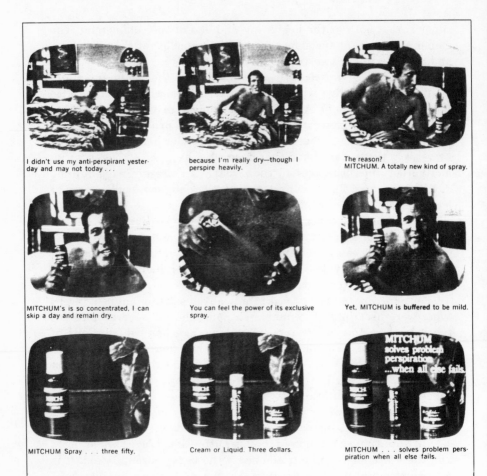

I didn't use my anti-perspirant yesterday and may not today . . .

because I'm really dry—though I perspire heavily.

The reason? MITCHUM. A totally new kind of spray.

MITCHUM's is so concentrated, I can skip a day and remain dry.

You can feel the power of its exclusive spray.

Yet, MITCHUM is **buffered** to be mild.

MITCHUM Spray . . . three fifty.

Cream or Liquid. Three dollars.

MITCHUM . . . solves problem perspiration when all else fails.

FOUR SUCCESSFUL USES OF POSITIONING

DRAMATIZATION OF A PROMISE

The commercial shown directly above helped triple sales of Mitchum's antiperspirants, doubling its share of the market in less than two years—even though Mitchum was priced at about three times the usual price of its leading competitors. What's more, this was accomplished with an advertising budget that was a fraction of the typical advertising budget of the leaders – but still in the multi-millions.

The product was distributed through both drugstores and food outlets. Consumer testing before advertising began showed that Mitchum was thought to be strong but gentle, and was considered superior.

The product was positioned as being right for people who perspire heavily, because this segment of the market had a high level of dissatisfaction with existing products, because Mitchum had the qualities to produce repeat sales with this group, and because advertising aimed at this group would affect normal users as well. A male model was used for greater identification by male viewers, and because women feel that men perspire more freely and would thus be convinced of the product's efficiency.

Note how the extra strength of Mitchum is not just stated but dramatized in the opening phrase in the commercial and the headline in the advertisement. Note too the prominence of the package, the repetition of the name in the commercial, and the use of the naked man to make it all memorable.

It was reported that many people hated this commercial – which is often true when a commercial is especially effective. The agency was S. R. Leon.

APPEALING TO THE BIG TICKET SEGMENT

The commercial on the following page may seem unspectacular, but it had spectacular results through the use of positioning. Note that the bank identifies itself as being right for businessmen – highly profitable customers who keep big deposit balances and sometimes take out big loans. Actual customers of the bank, like Mr. Arons, were used unrehearsed. The copywriting consisted largely in selecting appropriate parts of the many comments made and recorded. Five other commercials similar in nature were also made. The believability and the identification could hardly be stronger. The commercials were placed on stations listened to by a quality, male audience with a high percentage in managerial, professional, and executive occupations. Moderate frequency was used. Intensive frequency, right for package goods advertising, would have been wasteful. There are certain times

---

SOUND: BANK LOBBY SOUNDS UNDER.

ARONS: The feeling of walking in and just knowing everybody . . . and getting personalized service. But I was really impressed . . . (FADE UNDER)

ANNCR: Burt Arons, president, Tauber-Arons, tells why he likes to bank at Manufacturers.

ARONS: . . . and the people speak about . . . and really what they're saying is so true, about Manufacturers Bank, because there's really no bank in Los Angeles that you can walk into the front door and see the president sitting as you walk in. You know . . . and get a wave and so forth. The bank that I was at I didn't even know who the president was. I had no idea . . . you know . . . in some ivory tower some place. I think they're big enough to handle . . . (FADE UNDER)

ANNCR: Manufacturers. Not just another bank. Offices in downtown Los Angeles, Hollywood, Beverly Hills, San Fernando Valley, and Newport Beach. Manufacturers . . . member FDIC. Where business people have a good thing going.

ARONS: That's the best reference, to know that you've recommended somebody to somebody else and that they've now joined in together, and they've got a good thing going. It's the best bank in Los Angeles without a doubt.

---

when a man chooses a bank — when he's moved his residence or business, or when he's had an unfortunate experience with his present bank. Without these circumstances, or unless the bank has something better to offer — free gifts for opening an account, higher interest on deposits, or lower interest on loans — its impossible to cause a man to change banks. By spreading these commercials out over the target audience, the bank had the best chance of catching the attention of the highest number of businessmen and professionals who were thinking of opening an account at a bank and were undecided which to choose. In the first year of this campaign, 51% more new accounts were opened than in the previous year. The following year, new accounts were 62% higher. Note that this campaign was successful in

Los Angeles — an area where radio is more effective than in many other places in the United States because of the intensive use of automobiles. The agency was Gumpertz, Bentley, Fried, Scott.

ACCENTING A BENEFIT IGNORED BY THE LEADER

Diaparene Baby Wash Cloths, a late entry in the premoistened towelette category, had been advertised as a sanitary alternative to the wash cloth, with an added consumer benefit: convenience for mother.

BABY: You think this is the only place babies get messy?

Take it from me. We get messy all over.

Which is why Diaparene made Baby Wash Cloths.

They're moist, but not oily. So they really clean up.

And boy, are they soft.

Terrific for delicate skin. I use them all over.

I even take them on trips.

And if you think I like them, you should hear my mother.

WOMAN ANNCR: (VO) Diaparene Baby Wash Cloths with Lanolin. Because babies get messy all over.

The promise was similar to that offered by Wet Ones, the category leader, and Dabaways, the number three brand. A research study was conducted into consumer problems with premoistened towelettes. One particular problem surfaced: Many mothers perceived the existing products as unsuitable for use on baby's delicate skin. Reexamination of Diaparene Baby Wash Cloths uncovered an array of product attributes that could solve the problem. The sheets were soft, premoistened with lanolin, and contained no oil. The product was effective, yet mild enough to use all over a baby's body. The copy strategy adopted, therefore, stressed this *brand* advantage rather than the *product* advantage stressed by the leader and the rest of the competition.

Daytime television was used to reach mothers. For the first two months, the budget was $140,000, about one-tenth of the expenditure by all other brands of premoistened baby wipers combined. Diaparene's share of the market gained 2.3 percent. At the end of the year, Diaparene Baby Wash Cloths were clearly established as the fastest growing premoistened towelettes, with sales increasing at twice the category rate. The agency was BBDO.

COMPARATIVE ADVERTISING THAT WAS SAFE AND SUCCESSFUL

If you're not a plumber, the difference between a pipe-sealing compound and a thread-locking compound may seem insignificant. But it was all-important to the Loctite company in its promotion of Pipe Sealant with Teflon, a product that is better than anything else in preventing leaks in pipes. (Competitive products, for example, stop a leak only temporarily.) The initially proposed strategy seemed professionally logical—emphasize and dramatize the big dollar benefit that results from reducing the high cost of leaks.

However, analysis by Loctite and its advertising agency, Mintz & Hoke, Inc., of the *competition* and the *attitude of the audience* revealed that this strategy might fail, or would at best have only small success. The reason? Loctite had an excellent reputation as a producer of the thread-locking compound. So when the new pipe-sealing compound was described to prospective users in field research, they assumed it was a locking compound. Loctite to them was synonymous with thread-locking—and who can blame them? The ad-

LOCTITE
PST HERE

TAPE HERE

Loctite Pipe Sealant with Teflon stops leaks for good.

Even where tape fails.

- Loctite PST won't let fittings vibrate loose like tape—yet can be taken apart with a pipe wrench.
- Unlike tape, Loctite PST completely fills the "leak-paths" in threads to make a leak-proof seal—also prevents thread corrosion.
- Unlike tape, Loctite PST never shreds to contaminate system.
- Loctite PST seals instantly.
- Loctite PST is easy to apply.
- Loctite PST costs less per application than tape.

  Free sample and Leak Cost Calculator available—write Loctite Corporation, Newington, Connecticut 06111.

  "Stop Leaks" seminar available through your distributor. For his name and phone number, call toll-free 1-800-243-8810 (CT 1-800-842-8684).

LOCTITE®

* Reg. T.M. of Dupont Corp.
© 1977 Loctite Corporation

vertising therefore needed to make what Loctite Pipe Sealant does absolutely and dramatically clear. In addition, the advertising had to penetrate a market that was dominated by teflon tape. The market was satisfied with teflon tape because prospective users of Loctite's product didn't know any better.

The layout featured a pipe fitting, bold and dominant, to attract the attention of people interested in this subject. The name of the brand with its unique benefit was put in the headline and—this was key—a direct comparison was made with tape so there's no doubt about what Loctite Pipe Sealant does. Note that the comparison is made with another product, not another brand, so there is no danger of promoting the competition. One other key element in the construction of the advertising was the *purpose:* (a) to increase awareness and knowledge of Loctite Pipe Sealant among plant engineers, maintenance foremen, maintenance workers, and industrial distributors, and (b) to pull qualified sales leads. The copy therefore was full of additional benefits and ended with information telling where to write for a sample and with an illustration of the package. The layout is completely functional yet highly tasteful, different, and contemporary. The *nature of the audience* determined, in addition to the illustration, the media: *Plant Engineering, Industrial Equipment News, Chemical Engineering,* and *Hydraulics and Pneumatics.* Advertisements were placed monthly.

Within three months, 70 percent of the target audience specifically recalled seeing the ad. In two publications, the ad was not only the best read in its product category, but the best read in the issue.

The first insertion in one of the trade journals generated almost 1,500 responses. In addition, Loctite received nearly 500 personal letters from prospects requesting a salesman or samples and product information. Including letters and bingo card responses, over 7,000 inquiries were received in three months. One large prospect, who had previously resisted all Loctite sales efforts, switched from tape as a direct result of seeing the ad.

As a result of the advertising, sales promotion, and intensive sales efforts, sales increased 65 percent over the corresponding period of the previous year.

17

SUCCESS:
IF YOU DON'T MEASURE IT,
HOW DO YOU KNOW
IT EXISTS?

Direct response advertising created by experienced professionals fails less often than other types of advertising for two reasons. First, the principles are long established and well known by professionals. And second, the professionals are more careful about letting amateurs change the copy because they realize that the advertiser will know in a few days whether the advertising has been successful or not.

Other kinds of advertising fail more often than they succeed, usually because they are not measured objectively. As far as the advertising agency goes, it's often, "If the chief executive officer likes it, it's good advertising. If he doesn't, it's not." And the client's chief executive officer often likes the advertising if his wife, his associates, and the people at the club (who are often his competitors!) admire it.

Common Mistake #23: Putting pleasing the advertiser's chief executive officer ahead of creating effective advertising.

To cynical agency people and the chief executive's subordinates, it may seem practical to cater to his ego. It is, however, often shortsighted. If the advertising is ineffective, sooner or later the chief executive of the advertiser will become dissatisfied, the advertising agency will be fired, and the subordinates who went along with the ego-catering approach will suffer accordingly.

What is more, to be successful, the please-the-CEO approach, even over the short term, involves guessing what the chief executive will like. Whatever he tells the agency in advance may not be what he likes when he sees it executed in copy and art. Its ineffectiveness then becomes obvious to him, and he blames his advertising experts for not knowing better. One reason so many advertising executives have ulcers, drink too much, and even die earlier than their peers in other professions is because they practice the please-the-CEO method.

On the other hand, only a naive agency man ignores the prejudices, likes, and dislikes of those who approve the advertising. Ethical, intelligent agency people create advertising they believe will be effective, and then do their best to convince the advertiser of the worth of the advertising. The attitudes of the advertiser should affect the way the advertising is presented to him, not the advertising itself.

Establishing an objective measure of the advertising serves as a warning to the agency and as a restraint on self-indulgence by the advertiser.

Several ways of measuring the effectiveness of package goods and image advertising have been developed, but each method has its flaws. This doesn't mean that none should be used. It means that sensible people use them cautiously, with full knowledge of their limitations. There's the danger, too, that the agency will aim at creating ads that score high by the method used to measure, rather than at ads that will do the best job for the advertiser.

The most popular and widely-used method was developed by Daniel Starch. Interviewers knock on a number of doors all over the United States, asking people which ads they remember seeing and reading in a specific issue of a newspaper or magazine. One hundred people are interviewed for each issue covered — a small number when you consider that the results are projected as measurement of hundreds of thousands, sometimes millions of readers in each case!

Even so, Starch scores have provided the advertising profession with an invaluable tool, one which has resulted not only in the improvement of individual advertising campaigns but in the improvement of advertisements in general.

The Starch people are forthright about the limitations of their research. They state that measurements of a single advertisement placed once in a publication should be viewed with caution.

One other point should be noted about Starch scores. The higher an advertisement scores, the more trustworthy the results.

Suppose, for example, an advertisement scores 58 percent Noted,

55 percent Seen-Associated, and 12 percent Read Most. The meaning of these scores is as follows. If 58 out of the 100 people interviewed say they recognize and remember seeing the advertisement in the magazine, the score is 58 percent Noted. The signature or other indication of the name of the advertiser is covered when the ad is shown to the interviewees, so that asking the name of the advertiser can be a valid question. If 55 out of the 100 can remember who signed the advertisement, it has a 55 percent Seen-Associated score. Interviewees are also asked how much of the advertisement they read. If 12 out of the 100 say they read most of the advertisement, it has a score of 12 Read Most. If a different group of 100 were to be interviewed, the scores would probably differ by two, three, or four people. The 58 might be 62 or 54, the 55 might be 51 or 55, and the 12 might be 8 or 16. All of these — even the lower figures — are good scores.

Now let's take a lower-scoring ad: 21 percent Noted, 20 percent Seen-Associated, 4 percent Read Most. Mathematics experts say that 4 percent could actually mean as little as 1 percent or less, which is really terrible, or as much as 8 percent, which is pretty good. Four percent, in short, is too marginal a figure to be completely reliable.

Common Mistake #24: Not realizing the limitations of Starch advertising scores.

Note what the Starch score does *not* reveal. It does not tell whether the advertisement caused the reader to feel favorably toward the product or not. It does not tell whether it causes the reader to prefer the brand advertised. It does not tell how many readers actually bought the advertised product because of the advertisement.

The fact is, other research has shown that people who already use the brand or own the product remember the advertising better than non-owners! A widely-used brand will score higher than a new brand even though the new brand's advertising is superior.

As you can see, Starch scores are best used to partially measure the effectiveness of image advertising campaigns. They are worth little in direct response advertising because a well-written direct response advertisement usually does not appeal to a large percentage of the readers of a publication; the headline and/or illustration selects those who have need for the product. If a direct response ad is read by 5 percent of the readers of a publication with a million readers, and if one-fifth of those reading the advertisement respond, the advertiser would have 50,000 respondents — a very high return for any size direct response advertisement.

Starch scores are of some use in package goods advertising. If the interviewee remembers the ad and the brand advertised, it is also likely he will remember the promise or want to identify with the aura established by the advertisement — and so choose the brand.

One big agency, a giant in package goods advertising, has success-fully used a variant of the Starch method for years. It works like this: Members of a sample group are asked whether they remember the ad-vertising being tested, and then whether they are customers or not. Suppose 5 percent of those who do not remember the advertising are customers. This establishes a base for measuring the advertising, because we can assume that these are the people who would have bought the product anyway. If, say, 25 percent of those who *do* remember the advertising are customers, the conclusion is that 20 percent (25 percent less 5 percent) were influenced to become custom-ers by the advertising.

Maybe so, maybe not. Consider these points. First, customers tend to look at and remember advertising for the products they buy more than non-customers do. And second, this way of measuring fails to give credit to the art-that-conceals art kind of advertising, which causes prospective customers to vividly remember the brand and reasons for selecting it and to ignore the advertising that contains the message.

It is interesting to note that the agency using this testing method is particularly successful with pain-killers, where negative promise is the obviously correct appeal. The testing method checks how well the ad is remembered, not whether it is liked, admired, shows good taste, or is convincing. It is no coincidence that the advertisements created by this agency are often dramatically ugly — and remarkably effec-tive for certain products.

High Starch scores are often achieved by advertisements that fea-ture a large, dominating photograph, and below it a headline, short copy, and a signature in type about the same size as the headline. It's logical. People would rather look at photographs than at type, and the short copy gives a high Read Most score. Of course not just any photo-graph will do. The more dramatic and unusual it is, and the more center-oriented the photographic composition, the better, especially if it also features people.

Note, however, the dangers in creating advertisements to gain high Starch scores. The benefit may not be shown at its best through a photograph. Endeavoring to make the photograph interesting may distract readers from the product. It may be more desirable to cause more people to read the entire advertisement, in which case a different layout — one with illustrations scattered through the text — may be more desirable.

To counter these dangers, competing methods similar to but slightly different from Starch's have been developed. They cost more because more questions are asked and more people are interviewed. In addition to questions that are similar to Starch's, the interviewee is also asked what sales points he remembers.

As you might expect, the typical high-scoring Starch layout doesn't score highest when recall of sales points is the criterion. One of the highest scoring formats for sales points recall features before-and-after photographs, side by side.

However, just because an interviewee recalls the sales points doesn't mean he's convinced. In fact, another testing method that does measure conviction shows no correlation between recall of sales points and belief in them. Again it is not difficult to see why. The number of sales points may be unimportant. A single sales point may be more convincing than three, depending on its content. And for an interviewee to be able to repeat a sales point simply means that it's memorable, not that it's convincing.

Variants of these methods have been developed for television. One hundred or more homes are telephoned and viewers are asked whether they remember a certain commercial. They are then asked if they remember any benefits the brand offered.

Note further that any advertising that bases its appeals on identification will score low on sales point recall. The questions won't reveal that the advertisement made the interviewer *feel* he'd like to be associated with that brand or company.

Sophisticated methods of testing television commercials have been developed that go beyond recall of sales points and do give some measure of belief. Viewers may be invited to a theater or to a trailer parked near a supermarket. In effect, they are first given a choice of the brand to be tested and another brand, then shown a commercial and asked which brand they'd like to have.

Two techniques are ordinarily used to avoid interviewees knowing what is going on and therefore responding so as to please the testers rather than their own preferences.

One is the technique of matched samples. Suppose two hundred women are admitted to the trailer. The first is given a choice of brands without seeing the commercial, the second is given a choice after seeing the commercial, and so on until 50 have made a choice without advertising influence and 50 with. The first group is the control group.

A second technique is to ostensibly be testing a *program*. The interviewees are shown a pilot program and asked their opinion. Included in the pilot is the commercial being tested. All of the questions are about the program. Several brands of the product are on hand, and each interviewee is offered one as a reward for taking the time to view the program and give an opinion. Actually all that counts is which brand of the product each interviewee chooses as a reward.

Unfortunately, this kind of testing is not feasible for print advertising, driving some print advertisers to other methods.

Successful package goods advertisers often check and compare the effectiveness of different print campaigns, or of TV versus print, or of varying mixtures of media by using local newspapers and stations. A possible pattern is to choose six cities matched by similarity of demographics. One campaign is placed in two cities, a second campaign in a second two, and a third pair are used for control purposes. Stores are stocked with the brand so that sales can be monitored. At least two cities are used for each campaign in order to lessen the possibility of some outside factor affecting sales.

This method of testing measures the effectiveness of the entire marketing cycle – packaging, choice of type of store, specific stores, and areas within stores where the brand is displayed. And it's expensive. But it is very much worthwhile when an advertiser contemplates investing several millions of dollars in a national campaign.

The telephone booth commercial that appears in Chapter 15 used this method in a simplified way. Its purpose was to cause people to look up numbers themselves. In one marketing area only the commercial was run. In a second area, information operators were instructed to jog anyone asking for a number with a phrase such as, "Did you know you could look that number up, sir?" In a third area both methods were used – the commercial appeared and the operators jogged the users of the telephone. And in a fourth area nothing was done; this was the control group.

The results showed that the commercial alone did better than the instructions to the operators alone, but that the best results were obtained when the commercial was combined with that gentle nudge from the operators. And that was the method applied throughout the system.

One successful cosmetic package good advertiser has discovered an inexpensive method of testing that works for him. He tests his ads by modifying the ending of the proposed package goods advertisement to include a coupon. If the advertisement pulls well, he then uses it with a different package goods type ending. It works for him for the following reasons. First, the advertisements are designed on sound package goods principles, not on direct response principles. He and his advertising associates are experienced enough to know the difference. And second, the advertisement doesn't need to pay for itself. That is, it doesn't have to pull sufficient responses to make it as successful as a direct response advertisement. All it has to do is pull well by the standards he has established through experience. (Advertisers who want to sell cosmetics profitably by direct response feature prices.)

This method may work for this advertiser because younger women know how important their looks are. A woman's beauty is her power. Trivial differences therefore won't work in cosmetics advertising. Or perhaps it might be said that differences in cosmetics which may appear trivial to a man are not trivial to a woman. Consequently qualities in a cosmetic that make for brand differentiation can have sufficient power to elicit some direct response.

The Focus Group Interview is a popular copy research technique. Half a dozen people or more, selected as typical consumers of the product to be advertised, are gathered in a room. They are shown several of the proposed advertisements and asked to comment. Their comments are recorded and analyzed by a skilled copy researcher.

It is amazing how often some advertisements are misinterpreted. As you might expect, advertisements that use positive identification score very well. As one advertising man experienced in these interviews remarked, "If you went by focus interviews, Chivas Regal is not only the leading Scotch, it's numbers one through ten." In focus interviews the people tend to make comments they think will cause other members of the group to admire them. They are not interpreting the ad; they are reacting to one another and the Focus Group leader.

This is not to say focus interviews are worthless. At the minimum, they give some objective measure of what the advertising communicates. Agencies who sincerely want to do a good job for their clients often like focus interviews, because they help the agency eliminate ads or parts of ads that are inspired by the ego of the advertiser rather than needs of the advertising. The phrase "We are proud of our . . ." would draw scorn from a focus interview group.

Chief executive officers of advertisers like focus interviews because they prevent advertisements that might harm the company from being published. Subordinates of certain kinds of chief executive officers like focus interviews, despite their limitations, because the subordinates are thus partially relieved from negating absurd suggestions from the chief executive officer and other powerful figures in the company.

So focus interviews are here to stay, despite the fact that they measure neither the attention-getting ability of an advertisement nor its convincing power, and usually mask the power of ugly and negative-promise advertisements.

Focus interviews are most useful for pretesting image advertising, because advertising that won't cause the company to be admired is thus eliminated. They may be of some use in package goods advertising, particularly when a new product is being introduced, because interviewers can find out which aspects of the new product are regarded most highly. In direct response advertising, focus interviews are not worth the money. It's a cheaper and better test simply to try out advertisements in inexpensive media and see how they pull. Actually the most widespread and successful use of focus interviews is in market research – before any advertising has been created. Entirely new products and services have been inspired by the suggestions by consumers in focus groups.

The pulling power of direct response advertisements can be accurately compared by using split runs or regional editions of publications.

A run is split when alternative copies of a publication contain different advertisements. This is possible in publications that print two copies of each page at the same time. Both master forms are usually the same, but in this case each contains a different advertisement. Thus half the readers get the publication with Ad A, and the other half get the identical publication with Ad B. Since the publication is evenly distributed, there is no distortion of audience composition. The coupons are coded so that it is easy to count the coupons received from each advertisement and know which pulls better.

Regional editions of publications can be used in a similar manner.

One of two advertisements to be compared is placed in, say, the Eastern edition of a publication, and the other in the Western edition. If the costs are different for the two editions, the number of coupons received from each can be counted and divided into the cost of its edition. The costs-per-inquiry can then be compared.

The results may be distorted, however, because the audiences in the two areas are not strictly comparable. This can be compensated for by running the advertisements in the regional editions again, but reversing their places.

Suppose, for example, that in December Ad #1 is placed in the Eastern edition and Ad #2 in the Western edition. And the costs of the editions are the same. The results might be as follows:

	Eastern	Western
Ad #1	60	
Ad #2		40

It cannot be confidently deduced from this that Ad #1 is superior to Ad #2. It might be that the Eastern edition pulls better than the Western edition. It might be that reversing the advertisements in the January edition would give the following results:

	Eastern	Western
Ad #1		20
Ad #2	55	

(It would not be unusual for a repetition of the offer to result in lower returns in each case.)

If we combine the results, we get the following:

	Eastern	Western	Total Coupons Received
Ad #1	60	20	80
Ad #2	55	40	95

It would thus be shown that Ad #2 is superior to Ad #1.

Image advertising campaigns can be measured through the use of awareness-and-attitude studies. The target audience is surveyed as to their knowledge of the company and their attitudes toward it before any advertising appears, and again afterward. The big advantage is that the company really knows how it stands. The disadvantage is that it may not be the advertising that pushes the company's image up or down. To take an extreme possibility, let's say certain company officials are indicted just before the second study is made. The advertising may have been great but the test scores would indicate otherwise. Another disadvantage can be time. Ordinarily it takes a year or two for an image campaign to show much effect. It doesn't pay to test too early, and yet a lot of money can be wasted on advertising in a year.

Before-and-after surveys can be taken in three ways: through in-person interviews, by telephone, and by mail. The advantage of in-person interviews is that more questions can be asked, they can be more detailed, and answers can be followed up. The advantage of mail surveys is their cost is the lowest. Telephone surveys fall somewhere in between, both in cost and in the amount of information that can be gathered.

It is vital that any survey be made under the supervision of, or at least in consultation with, a research professional. One common mistake made by amateurs conducting mail surveys is this: they believe that the larger the number of people mailed to, the more reliable the results. Some Congressmen, for example, mail survey questionnaires to everyone in their districts and then tabulate the answers, even though a very small percentage—10 percent, even 1 percent—answer the questionnaire. The answers only indicate what is felt by those who feel most strongly about politics and current questions. Their answers are not a reliable measure of what the constituency believes.

In a mail survey, reliability of the results depends on the percentage of those who answer the survey. If, say, 50 percent of those mailed to answer, it can't be assumed that the remaining 50 percent would answer in the same proportion. This has been proved time and again by telephoning those who did not answer mail surveys. The people who do *not* answer are different from those who *do* answer—that's one reason they didn't answer.

Look at it this way: A bag contains, say, one thousand marbles, some of them black, some white. The problem is to estimate how many of each color are in the bag. Just looking at the marbles on top won't give a reliable indication, because all those of one color may have been placed in the bag at the same time, blacks on the bottom, whites on top. Looking only at the marbles on top—distorting the sample by doing what's easiest—is equivalent to assuming that those few who answer a survey are representative of everyone else.

An experienced, competent research professional can help determine the least expensive method possible for the results desired, decide on the number of people who must be interviewed so the results will be reliable, help draft the questionnaire so that respondents are not pushed to answer one way or another, and draft a covering letter that will result in a high percentage of answers.

Do the many limitations mean that copy testing is not worthwhile?

Copy testing can't create great advertising but it can prevent a company from continuing to place advertising that is ineffective or harmful.

Starch studies can show an image advertiser whether his advertisements are getting any attention. If his ads are continually below average compared to advertisements for companies in the same industry, he should consider taking action of some kind: asking for a new creative approach, asking for new creative people on the account, or changing agencies.

An awareness-and-attitude study can help. The advance study can show the advertiser where he stands, and may be helpful in determining both the budget and the creative approach. If he's behind his competitors and he wants to close the gap, a big budget and a highly provocative advertising campaign are indicated. If he's on top, a more conservative budget and creative approach may be appropriate.

The after-study can show the image advertiser whether he's on the right track or not. He can salt the results with the favorable or unfavorable publicity the company has been getting in the news columns and on the air, and judge whether he's getting his money's worth.

As we have seen, the package goods advertiser has a variety of testing techniques to choose from. The bigger the advertising budget, the more elaborate and reliable the techniques he can afford to use.

The direct response advertiser can, at the minimum, keep records and look at the results. And he can use split runs to compare results from different advertisements.

No advertising campaign of any real size – say, $250,000 a year or more – should be undertaken without some objective measure of the results. Some years ago psychologists at Princeton conducted a test proving that people aiming at a target did better if they were told how well each shot placed than if they continued to shoot without knowing the results. It is almost impossible for advertising to improve if the advertiser and the agency don't objectively know how effective – or ineffective – it really is. **Common Mistake #25: Having no objective measure of the advertising's effectiveness.**

WHICH APPLIANCE AD ATTRACTED MORE READERS?

The advertisements on the facing page were tested by Daniel Starch & Staff for the three categories of readership: Noted, or the percentage of readers who remembered seeing the ad; Seen-Associated, or the percentage who saw the part of the ad that clearly indicated the advertiser; and Read Most, the percentage who read 50 percent or more of the text. Ad A appeared in four colors in the May issue of *Reader's Digest*, Ad B in four colors in the November issue of the same year. Readership among women was recorded separately from readership among men. The results are shown on the next page.

WHAT COPY-TESTING SHOWED

Noted	Ad A	Ad B
Men	30%	25%
Women	61%	48%

Ad A scored higher in Noted for both men and women, because photographs, particularly of food, generally attract more attention than do cartoons. The ad was noted by about twice as many women as men largely because of the nature of the product. This factor also caused readership of this ad to fall off more rapidly among men than among women.

Read Most	Ad A	Ad B
Men	3%	8%
Women	18%	19%

The continuing story told by the series of illustrations caused more of those who noticed Ad B to continue reading it, so that Read Most for women is statistically the same for both ads. (Differences of one or two percentage points are meaningless when only 100 people are interviewed.) The entertainment quality of Ad B may have contributed to holding more male readers. Even more important – the benefits in Ad B appeal to men.

The Seen-Associated score for women was higher for Ad A, which is usual, since Seen-Associated scores usually follow the Noted scores if the advertiser's name is sufficiently displayed.

Seen-Associated	Ad A	Ad B
Men	18%	19%
Women	58%	41%

The Seen-Associated score for men was about the same for both ads, probably because the illustrations in Ad B made more men move their eyes downward to the logo.

WHICH GAINES-BURGER AD ATTRACTED MORE READERS?

The only important difference between the two advertisements on the following pages is the addition of the store coupon. Only a few words in the copy and the type size are different. Both full-color, one-page bleed advertisements appeared in *Sunset* magazine. The ad with the coupon appeared in August 1972, the other in November 1972. Was there any difference in the Noted, Seen-Associated, and Read Most Starch scores? If so, which did better – and why?

The way people feel about cheeseburgers, dogs feel about Cheese Flavor Gaines·burgers.*

Remember how terrific it was when you discovered that hamburgers didn't always have to be just hamburgers?

Ah, cheeseburgers! People are crazy about them.

And strange as it may sound, we've found a lot of dogs who are just as crazy about having cheese along with their burger.

So we're introducing Cheese Flavor Gaines·burgers.*

They've got real cheese added to the good meaty taste of the regular burger. (Which is something you won't find in any can.)

They've got all the nutrition that regular Gaines-burgers have.

With beef by-products, beef, vegetable protein and all the vitamins and minerals a dog needs to stay good and healthy.

And they've got all the convenience of regular Gaines·burgers. No odor, no can, and no leftovers to store.

Ask your dog if he likes new Cheese Flavor Gaines·burgers.

Years from now, he'll look back and remember the day he found out burger didn't always have to be just burger.

And he'll love you for it.

The way people feel about cheeseburgers, dogs feel about Cheese Flavor Gaines·burgers.*

Remember when you first tasted cheese on a hamburger? Ah…Cheeseburgers! No wonder people are crazy about them.

And strange as it may sound, we've found a lot of dogs who are just as crazy about having cheese along with their burger. So we're introducing Cheese Flavor Gaines·burgers.*

They've got real cheese added to the good meaty taste of the regular burger.

They've got all the nutrition that regular Gaines·burgers have. With beef by-products, beef, vegetable protein and all the vitamins and minerals a dog needs to stay good and healthy.

And they've got all the convenience of regular Gaines·burgers. No odor, no can, and no leftovers to store.

Ask your dog if he likes new Cheese Flavor Gaines·burgers.

Years from now, he'll look back and remember the day he found out burger didn't always have to be just burger.

And he'll love you for it.

The cheese taste makes the burger taste better.

*Ingredients: Beef By-Products and Beef, Soy Grits, Sucrose, Soy Flour, Soy Protein Concentrate, Dehydrated pasteurized process Cheddar and Blue Cheese.

WHAT COPY-TESTING SHOWED

Both advertisements scored well on Noted and Seen-Associated, which is not surprising considering that both use a rectangular human-interest photograph and both show the name of the product in the headline. Advertising people with a little knowledge may be surprised at the Read Most scores. Conventional wisdom, borne out by Starch tests on thousands of advertisements, says that ads with coupons are *less* well read than those without — even though advertisements with coupons generally draw more responses. Nobody knows for sure the reason for this paradox. According to one line of reasoning, the coupon attracts the kind of reader apt to send in for a free booklet or other offer but drives away some of those who just want information. If this is true, it might be supposed that the ad without a coupon would be better read than the one with the coupon, but the reverse was the case. Approximately six times as many people read most of the copy of the ad with the coupon. Here are the scores:

	With Coupon	Without Coupon
Noted	57%	40%
Seen-Associated	40%	28%
Read Most	12%	2%

A rationale for the higher readership of the ad with the coupon is as follows: The reader is attracted by the photograph, reads the headline, and then his or her eye jumps down to the coupon and the words, "Save 15¢." These two words drive the reader back up into the copy to find out how to save that 15¢. However, this is after-the-fact reasoning. It would have been impossible to know in advance which ad would be better read without the invaluable aid of the Starch scores. The advertising agency was Young & Rubicam.

WHICH ELMER'S GLUE TV COMMERCIAL WAS BETTER REMEMBERED?

The commercials on the following pages, created by Conahay & Lyon, were tested by Burke Marketing Research, Inc. Burke telephones people in test cities the day after the commercial appears. The interviewer first determines whether the interviewee has seen the program in which the test commercial was telecast. The usual sample size is 200, which yields a commercial audience of between 140 and 160. (The number is less than 200 because some people leave the room when the commercial is on or change the channel. Scores are reported as a percentage of the commercial audience.

BORDEN CHEMICAL

Elmer's Glue-All

"Hammock"   30 Seconds

ANNCR: (VO) You are about to see . . .

a demonstration . . . of strength.

The strength and versatility of Elmer's Glue-All.

We're gluing leather strips to canvas . . .

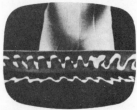

to show you that Elmer's . . .

is the glue with strength to spare . .

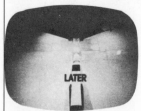

for just about any household job you've got to glue.

(MUSIC UNDER)
ANNCR: Here we go.

(MUSIC UNDER)

(MUSIC UNDER)

Holding power . . . to spare!

That's what made Elmer's Glue-All . . . America's favorite glue.

BORDEN CHEMICAL

Elmer's Glue-All

"Diving Board" 30 Seconds

ANNCR: (VO) This is a demonstration . . .

of strength.

The remarkable strength . . .

of Elmer's Glue-All.

Watch.

You see, Elmer's is stronger than . . .

most any of those . . .

household jobs you'll ever have to do.

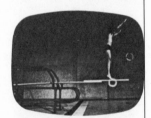

And when you're . . .

stronger than the jobs you have to do . . .

you get to be America's favorite glue.

Elmer's Glue-All.

WHAT COPY-TESTING SHOWED

Both commercials scored well compared with the average commercial. The norm for females is 23 percent, according to Burke. "Hammock" was recalled by 26 percent of the women, "Diving Board" by 34 percent. The Burke norm for males is 20 percent. "Hammock" scored 31 percent, "Diving Board" 39 percent among men. So "Diving Board" is clearly the superior commercial so far as recall is concerned.

18

THE FUNDAMENTAL MISTAKE
BEGINNERS MAKE
WITH DIRECT MAIL

There is no obvious economic incentive for an advertiser to use an agency for direct mail. Every last thing, especially the copywriting, must be paid for. Consequently, many advertisers choose to do their own direct mail. Sometimes this is an excellent idea if the company does enough direct mail to warrant employing the necessary experts.

Because experts are necessary. A direct mail letter often looks deceptively simple. Anybody can write a letter, can't they?

The fact is that an effective direct mail letter differs greatly from an ordinary letter. The purpose of most ordinary letters is simply to inform – to communicate certain facts and/or ideas to the recipient. It's a one-to-one relationship, and if the writer's meaning is clear, the letter will be 100 percent effective.

The purpose of a direct mail letter, on the other hand, is to get action – to make at least some of the recipients do what the advertiser wants. And the relationship is not one-to-one. The writer must imagine what those who receive the letter are like, how much they already know of the subject, what their attitude toward it is, and so on. Yet he can't just aim at the average. He's really hoping to influence only a small percentage of the addressees. Generally a return of one-half of one percent is satisfactory – one percent is excellent – depending on the cost of the mailing, the price of what is being sold, and the profit margin.

In other words, a direct mail letter sent to a list of 10,000 really is aiming at 50 or 100 addressees who can be sufficiently aroused to answer the letter by mail or telephone and perhaps send money. To do this, a direct mail letter must arouse emotion. It must make some of its readers want what is being offered enough to overcome their natural lethargy and their natural inclination not to part with their money. In fact, an effective direct mail letter is often, but not always, so strong that it would be offensive on a one-to-one basis.

It takes a distinct type of talent and personality to write a direct mail letter that pulls profitably – someone who knows that people respond principally to appeals to their greed and to their fears, someone who can write clearly and logically, and who knows how to arouse emotion with facts.

That's one kind of expert an advertiser needs if he's going to handle his own direct mail. Another kind is the direct mail administrator. He selects the lists of people to be mailed to. This is of primary importance since some lists are much more fruitful than others, and some can prove a waste of money.

He also keeps records. First, he keeps records in order to see if the concept of direct mail for the product or service being offered is likely to be profitable. Nobody knows what can or cannot be sold by direct mail. Automobiles have been sold, as have insurance, securities, land, wallets, magazine subscriptions, books, lobsters, fruit, credit cards, cutlery, education – the list is virtually endless. He also keeps records in order to improve profitability. He designs tests of mailing lists, of copy approaches and of other variants, such as type of reply card, elaborateness of enclosure, and class of postage.

Successful direct mail programs are built, not created immediately. While experts can make better judgments than non-experts, nobody can tell in advance what kind of letter will pull best for a specific product or service, or what kind of list is going to work best. Once an advertiser finds from his records that he has a mailing that pulls, he can use it to test other lists of addressees. And he can have other letters and enclosures written and designed, and test them against the successful letter and enclosures.

A direct mail administrator knows how to keep the records and how to calculate profitability. He may even, from his experience, be a good judge of what kinds of letters and enclosures will pull well, but he seldom is a good writer of direct mail copy himself. He necessarily has a different kind of personality, and his background will normally be quite different. He is a numbers man, while a copywriter is a word man.

All too often, however, the advertiser hires one man to do both jobs – with the result that the direct mail program either is not profitable or not as profitable as it could be. Sometimes the advertiser tries to do the entire job himself, with even more disastrous results.

Common mistakes made by amateurs doing their own direct mail include:

Mailing on Friday. There's a natural tendency to clean up work by the end of the week. Also, if mail is going coast to coast, conscientious executives want to mail on Friday to reduce the number of business days lost. The fact is that Friday is the worst day to send out mailings to businesses, and sometimes the worst for home-addressed mailing as well. Higher returns from business-addressed mail result when the mail is received on Tuesday, Wednesday or Thursday. A businessman has much more mail to get through on Monday, so he will devote less time to anything new. On Fridays, he's anxious to finish up – is less likely to be receptive to a new idea. Home mailings received on Friday or Saturday are most fruitful, since the recipients have plenty of time to read, think, answer. A letter mailed on Friday *may* arrive Saturday, but with the present deterioration of mail service, why take a chance?

Sending material that is too impersonal. Novices in direct mail often so much want to look professional that while what is sent is slick and glossy it does not move many of the recipients to act. Generally, the closer a communication resembles a personal letter, the more the responses. More specifically, a letter with the name of the addressee at the beginning will pull better than one headed "Dear Friend." A letter with the recipient's name in the body copy, even though it is obviously typed by computer, will pull better than without; a letter with the signature in different ink from the black of the typewritten words will pull better. The more personal, caring, and direct the tone, the greater the number of responses. Even hand-written corrections of typewritten mistakes can up responses. Sometimes novices send a booklet alone, without a covering letter. A letter without an enclosure is often effective; an enclosure without a letter, seldom. Generally it is most effective to enclose a letter, booklet, or folder along with a self-addressed reply card, although additional enclosures can be effective for some mailings.

Not making it easy for addressees to respond. Responses can be increased by enclosing a reply card, even more if the card or enclosed envelope is already self-addressed and stamped. Even better is the reply card on which the addressee's name is already printed, so that all he or she need do is drop it in a mail box.

These and other mistakes made by beginners in direct mail result from one overriding mistake, **Common Mistake #26: An advertiser handling direct mail himself without retaining the necessary experts.**

ARE ADVERTISING AGENCIES OVERPAID?

Often, the best strategy for a big package goods advertiser is to spend millions of dollars on a single commercial, to keep running that same commercial over and over until every television viewer is sick and tired of it – and then to run it some more.

This is highly lucrative for the advertising agency. On billings of $10 million, the advertising agency gets $1,500,000. Even when the agency throws in a considerable amount of free research and other services, its profits are likely to be enormous. Yet if the advertising increases sales by several times $10 million, is the agency being overpaid? What is the right price for a single great advertising creation? It is more difficult to evaluate than the Mona Lisa.

In actual practice, the payments to agencies with accounts of this size are determined not on moral or abstract grounds, but through the pull and tug of intelligent business practice.

Some years ago the big profits that agencies were making on sizable TV accounts caused the usual agency compensation system to come under attack. Advertisers saw the huge amounts agencies were netting, and resented it. Advertisers couldn't save any money by placing advertising directly with the networks, because the networks charged them the established rate. Agencies are traditionally recompensed by paying the media 15 percent less than the established rate, which is the amount they bill advertisers.

Two special kinds of agencies sprang up to capitalize on the advertisers' desire to get more for their money. One kind, the time-buying agency, may save an advertiser money simply by billing the client for less than the established rate, say 10 percent off, thereby reducing the agency's commission to 5 percent. Or the time-buying agency may give the advertiser more spots for the same budget, again reducing agency commission. This agency might save its client even more money through adept bargaining skills. TV networks and stations are susceptible to bargaining, because time is a wasting asset – if they don't sell it, they can't keep it in inventory.

Time-buying agencies, however, did not supply creative services. So another kind of agency developed at the same time – the advertising boutique, which wrote and designed commercials for a fixed fee. The advertisers saved money, because even though the fees of the boutiques look high in dollars – say $50,000 for a single commercial – the amount may be low as a percent of the time cost. Let's suppose $1 million is to be spent running a single commercial. The normal commission to the agency would be $150,000. If the time-buying agency takes only a 5 percent commission ($50,000) and creative costs are $50,000, the advertiser saves $50,000 – a small amount as a percent of billings but perhaps enough to pay the advertising manager's salary.

Some advertisers who switched to the combination of boutique and time-buying agencies returned after a while to using full-service agencies. The reasons are hidden in carefully-worded press releases, but it is likely that in some cases advertisers found the old 15 percent system didn't really overpay the agency when the results were considered. In other instances, the full-service agency simply took less than 15 percent and rebated the excess to the advertiser in one way or another.

Anyhow, it is doubtful that any agency with big-budget clients is overpaid for more than a brief period. The competition is too keen. Big-budget advertisers can afford to pay sufficiently big salaries to their advertising people so they can hire some of the most competent professionals – men who have been on the agency as well as the client side, and who know how to squeeze a dollar ten's worth of work out of the agency for every dollar of agency income.

The commonest mistake, as far as agency payments are concerned, is made not by advertisers with big budgets, but by advertisers with small ones. And the smaller the budget, the bigger the mistake. A small-budget advertiser labors under a double handicap. His advertising will tend to gain less attention and be less well remembered (or get fewer responses) because of smaller size and/or frequency, and the people creating his advertising are paid considerably less.

It's always possible for a poorly-paid copywriter to come up with an advertisement as effective as one created by a well-paid copywriter, but it's not something that can be counted on to happen continually. Capable copywriters and art directors move up the wage scale rapidly — more rapidly than competent people do in other professions.

For small and moderate budgets, there's not much cushion left for creative salaries after other expenses are taken care of. Here's how the costs break down for a typical agency. (Percentages vary from agency to agency.)

Advertising Budget		100.0%
Media		85.0
Available for advertising agency		15.0
Non-payroll expenses	3.7	
U.S. income taxes, pensions	1.5	
Profit after taxes	.8	
Total	6.0	
Available for payroll		9.0
Account executives, planning	3.0	
Production	1.6	
Accounting, general office, research, new business, supervisory salaries	2.2	
Total	6.8	
Available for copy and art		2.2%

As you can see, only a little over 2 percent of the advertising budget is usually available for creativity — and at some agencies it's even less. On a million-dollar budget, about $22,000 is thus available for creative work; on a half-million-dollar budget, $11,000; on a $100,000 budget, $2,200; and on a $50,000 budget, only $1,100. Since several advertisements are normally needed, even the million-dollar budget does not leave an enormous sum for the copywriter, copy supervisor, copy director, art director, assistant art director, and creative director.

A small-budget advertiser can greatly increase the amount of time, effort, and talent that will be devoted to creating his advertising by just a slight increase in his budget.

Take a $50,000 advertising budget. Suppose a $5,000 creative fee is paid the agency, increasing the budget only 10 percent to $55,000. The $1,100 that the agency would normally devote to creative costs is increased to $6,100 — as much as is normally available from a $280,000 budget. That gives five times as much for creativity with only a 10 percent budget increase.

The small-budget advertiser who pays a creative fee can logically expect that each of his advertisements will successfully compete with other advertising for attention, memorability, readership, and/or responses.

20

SIX MISTAKES MADE
BY CRITICS OF
ADVERTISING

Read this chapter even if you couldn't care less about social issues. It will serve as a partial review, throw additional light on certain principles previously discussed, and put your understanding of advertising on a sound theoretical foundation.

1. *"Advertising makes people buy things they don't need."*

This criticism is partly true, but mostly false, and the false part has not been widely refuted for an interesting reason.

   The criticism is true to the extent that advertising causes people to buy things they wouldn't otherwise think they need. Does anybody "need" TV dinners, deodorants, a smoother shave, stylish clothes, an automobile one is proud to own, blenders and other electric appliances, longer, thicker eyelashes, soap that cleans dishes without aging hands? How do you define "need"?

   There's little question that advertising increases the desire for material things. Advertising and mass production go hand in hand. Mass production calls for high initial fixed costs. Once an automobile plant is tooled up to produce 100,000 cars, each additional car produced and sold lowers the average cost of all cars produced by that plant. The more cars sold, the bigger the profit and/or the lower the selling price of each car. Generally, a lower selling price accompanies bigger profits because the lower the price, the greater the number of people who can afford to buy the car.

It is, therefore, good business for the mass producer to advertise not only to tell the masses what they can get, and at what price, but to create a concept of a better life. By raising some people's standards, advertising causes them to live better. And thus also benefits those who would buy the products anyway by making them available at lower prices.

Advertising, however, can't make people buy something they have no use for. The power of advertising has been much exaggerated. Anybody who has been responsible for advertising for any considerable length of time knows how difficult it is to mount a successful advertising campaign. Advertising copy that does not offer the consumer a psychological or physiological benefit will fail. And if a consumer responds to an advertised benefit, doesn't he by definition have a previous need?

Common Mistake #27: Believing advertising is more powerful than it really is.

It's a mistake made not only by critics of advertising but by many advertisers. It's the mistake that's behind the many advertising campaigns that try to do too much with too little. Ads are placed in too many publications with too little frequency, or if they are placed in only one publication, they are not run often enough to make an impression. And occasionally, an ad is too small to attract a good number of readers, or not big enough to convey the desired image.

People who make their living from advertising are not eager to correct this misconception, to counter the criticism that advertising makes people buy things they don't need. The accusation is a compliment to their power. Why should those who profit most from the exaggerated conception of advertising power — people in broadcasting, publishers of newspapers and magazines, ad agencies, and so on — disabuse potential advertisers? Do doctors deprecate the power of drugs?

2. *"Advertising makes products cost more."*

As we have seen, advertising as a modern economic institution causes products to cost less. (That's why the Soviet Union is belatedly introducing it.) But "How about cosmetics?" a knowing logician might interject. "Advertising expenditures sometimes are as much as 50 percent or more of production costs — and while cosmetics are mass-produced, sales volumes are not really sizable."

In these instances, customers are not only buying the product, they are buying associations that go with the product. The advertising does make the product cost more, but the consumer gets something more. In the case of cosmetics, she gets a feeling, an enjoyment, a confidence she wouldn't otherwise get. The advertising gives the product added value.

3. "Good restaurants don't advertise."

This critic is really saying: "If you've got a good product, you don't need to advertise." Actually, restaurants and similar establishments, where the sale of additional units does not increase profits after a certain point, are the exception that prove the rule. Restaurants that are turning away customers don't advertise because making more people want the product won't increase sales or profits. Their problem is capacity. In terms of maximizing profits, the owner made a mistake when he established it. If he'd made it bigger, he would have even bigger profits. Ideally, his restaurant should be full with nobody turned away.

So don't by-pass a restaurant because it advertises. The advertising may simply indicate that the owner was optimistic and tables are available. Anyone who uses the phrase, "Good restaurants don't advertise" to derogate advertising, simply does not understand the limiting effect capacity has on the profitability of advertising.

4. "Advertising is a bunch of lies."

There are laws against fraud. What's more, a number of institutions police advertising—most importantly, the Federal Trade Commission. Many publications and broadcasters won't accept advertising they believe claims more than the product can truly deliver.

Even if there were no restraints, however, fraudulent advertising would not prove profitable—and therefore would not continue—because of the following fact of life: Advertising that stresses a feature not possessed by the product is the most effective way to draw attention to that deficiency. If a soap is advertised as getting clothes white in cold water and it doesn't, consumers may buy the brand once but they won't buy it again.

Advertising doesn't police itself quite as effectively if the expenditure is large (automobiles, for example) or when the benefit is either hard to measure (investment advice) or is received long after purchase (insurance). In these instances, however, repeated disparities between the advertising and reality will be disastrous to the advertiser's reputation, and therefore to sales and profits. Of course, there are always some people who will buy products of this kind from companies that make unrealistic promises, but there's probably no way to protect fools.

Anytime anyone says, "Advertising is a bunch of lies," what he generally means is, "Advertising exaggerates," which it does—a sin that the critic himself is guilty of.

5. *"Advertising insults the intelligence."*

Package goods commercials in particular cause some viewers to feel that advertising insults their intelligence. After all, the advertising is trying to make them feel that a tiny difference in a low-priced product is important enough for them to remember the next day.

This criticism reveals the critic's ignorance. It's like criticizing a rock star for not being a concert pianist. Advertising intentionally does not aim at the consumer's intelligence, but at his emotions. A person acts and remembers because an emotion is aroused. Intelligence is negative and restraining.

6. *"I never buy anything because of the advertising."*

What he's really saying is that the exaggerated promises in package goods advertising don't affect him. It's always interesting to see what brands of liquor and cigarettes this critic uses and what make of car he owns. He's likely to be particularly suspectible to skilled identification advertising because he doesn't believe it's working.

A CAR CARD USES PROMISE TO GET RESPONSES

If it were not for advertising like the example on the following page, people would go on thinking that life insurance can be bought only from a life insurance salesman. And they would go on paying much more for their insurance.

Car cards are largely used to increase awareness of a product or service. However, they can be used, as the Ogilvy & Mather advertise-

ment on the facing page shows, to elicit direct responses. Tear-off business reply cards on hooks implemented a principle, previously discussed, that the easier the advertisement makes it for people to reply, the greater the number of responses. The headline directly features the promise – a big amount of insurance at low cost. The use of Joe DiMaggio helps increase responses in two ways: by adding credibility to the promise and by helping to make The Bowery the kind of bank New Yorkers would like to identify with. Including a man, a woman, and a child in the illustration increases the attention-getting power of the car card, improves identification, and shows the reason for the benefit (low-cost insurance for the family). The card appeared alternately in subways and buses, each time in one-half of all the vehicles in the five boroughs of New York. The cost was less than $100,000. The directly attributable results: 12,088 reply cards, 667 applications, $8 million in policies.

21

THE 27 MOST COMMON MISTAKES IN ADVERTISING AND HOW TO AVOID THEM: A REVIEW

Mistake #1. Putting in charge of advertising a person whose responsibilities do not coincide with the purpose of the advertising.

To avoid it: Define accurately the purpose of the advertising before selecting the person to be responsible, and/or have the chief executive officer retain responsibility for the advertising, assisted by an advertising manager with no other responsibilities.

Mistake #2. Choosing an advertising agency with the wrong expertise.

To avoid it: Ask prospective agencies about their experience with companies whose products and services are marketed the same way as yours.

Mistake #3. Trying to do too much with too few advertising dollars.

To avoid it: Look at case histories of successful advertising, note what was accomplished with how many dollars – and then be skeptical. Since companies and agencies tend to publish their most successful case histories, it's wise to assume that the results for dollars expended represent the upper limit.

Mistake #4. The advertiser doing too much of the agency's work.

To avoid it: Remember that one measure of an executive's capability is the quality or amount of work he can get out of subordinates and suppliers. And that there is no substitute for the agency's objectivity. Two quotations may help: "An attorney who conducts his own defense has a fool for a client." And:
"Oh wad some power the giftie gie us
To see oursels as others see us!
It wad frae monie a blunder free us,
An' foolish notion."

Mistake #5. Choosing a medium based on its low rate rather than on its cost per thousand readers, listeners, or viewers.

To avoid it: Compare audience sizes and responsiveness as well as cost.

Mistake #6. Not advertising frequently enough.

To avoid it: Remember that only a fraction of the readers, viewers, or listeners can recall seeing a specific advertisement or commercial by the next day. And that their memories become rapidly dimmer in the days that follow.

Mistake #7. Making an advertisement bigger than it need be.

To avoid it: While a large advertisement can create an impression impossible for a small one, remember that attention is gained at a diminishing rate once an advertisement does more than dominate the page.

Mistake #8. Expecting too much from creativity in copy and art.

To avoid it: Remember that the returns from a direct response advertisement are limited by what is being offered, and that there is no substitute for repeated impressions for memorability.

Mistake #9. Imitating instead of analyzing.

To avoid it: Remember that imitative advertising is seldom, if ever, effective. Instead of borrowing from others, be sure your advertising observes the six conditions: Purpose, Attitude of the Audience, Medium, Nature of the Audience, What Is Being Advertised, and Competition.

Mistake #10. Trying to gain attention by being different in form rather than in content.

To avoid it: Ask the following questions: "Will the beginning attract the attention of the target audience? Is it the kind of beginning that is most effective for what the audience is to do or feel? Will it arouse the most effective type of emotion toward the product, service, or company?"

Mistake #11. Creating for presentation, not for the medium.

The agency can avoid this one by educating account executives in the hazards of production. The advertiser can avoid this by asking when in doubt for final engraver's proofs on the same kind of stock as is used by the publication. Also by showing the final proof to an outspoken executive in the company who has not seen the layouts or the earlier proofs.

Mistake #12. Being over-creative with type.

To avoid it: Ask the question, "Is it easy to read?"

Mistake #13. Making the logo the wrong size.

To avoid it: Remember that in direct response advertising, the company name is generally unimportant; in corporate advertising, it is most important.

Mistake #14. Not concentrating the advertising on the reader, listener, or viewer.

To avoid it: Remember that what interests people most is themselves.

Mistake #15. Making fun of the prospect.

To avoid it: Try to remember when *you* ever enjoyed being laughed at.

Mistake #16. Using a pun in the headline.

To avoid it: Remember that it is difficult to find a provenly-successful advertisement, or even one that has won an award, with a pun in the headline.

Mistake #17. Entertaining instead of selling.

To avoid it: Picture a salesman in a Las Vegas nightclub trying to explain the virtues of a new type of steel to a prospect while naked girls are parading a few feet away.

Mistake #18. Failing to sufficiently arouse the right kind of emotion.

To avoid it: Remember that the key emotions are hope, admiration, and fear.

Mistake #19. Applying a sound copy principle at the wrong time.

To avoid it: Check the copy and art against the six determinants: Purpose, Attitude of the Audience, Medium, Nature of the Audience, What Is Being Advertised, and Competition.

Mistake #20. Failing to fully utilize the peculiar advantages of the medium, especially television.

To avoid it: If the same message is to appear in different media, be sure the advertisements and commercials are written by copywriters who are skilled in the appropriate medium.

Mistake #21. Failing to capitalize on the inherent nature of the product, service, or company.

To avoid it: The advertising agency should carefully study the product, service, or company. The agency has the advantage of objectivity.

Mistake #22. Promoting the sale of a competitor's brand.

To avoid it: Develop a distinctive competitive benefit, establish a distinctive image, or develop a strong position strategy.

Mistake #23. Putting pleasing the advertiser's chief executive officer ahead of creating effective advertising.

An agency may avoid this mistake by adhering to appropriate polices; an advertiser avoids it simply by establishing an objective measure of the advertising's effectiveness. Personal pride or firm ethical attitudes may make it easy for some individuals to avoid it. Others may be guided by what is likely to prove most efficacious over the long term—or even by what may be best for their own physical and mental health.

Mistake #24. Not realizing the limitations of Starch advertising scores.

To avoid it: Remember that the Starch organization itself states that its scores on a single advertisement are not reliable. And remember that Starch scores don't measure persuasiveness.

Mistake #25. Having no objective measure of the advertising's effectiveness.

To avoid it: Settle on a method by which the advertising is to be measured before any appears.

Mistake #26. An advertiser handling direct mail himself without retaining the necessary experts.

To avoid it: Remember that direct mail is not necessarily cheap, particularly if a booklet is enclosed. If it costs $10,000 to mail to 10,000 names and a 1 percent response results, the cost per response is $100. Experts can cut costs and increase responses.

Mistake #27. Believing advertising is more powerful than it really is.

To avoid it: Discover what it takes for advertising to succeed.

22
WHY SOME ADVERTISING SUCCEEDS

For the advertiser, the most critical decisions are: (1) choosing an agency, and (2) approving the agency's recommendation of media, copy, and art (or disapproving or asking for modifications). It is an understatement to note that these are also critical points for the advertising agency.

This book has attempted to furnish not only facts, but a comprehensive analysis of advertising, so that, at the critical times, corporate executives can make sound decisions and agency people can make better recommendations. This final chapter will provide corporate executives and agency people with tools and additional information that will help them use what has gone before most effectively.

Successful advertising is seldom a matter of luck, inspiration, or even genius. Sometimes success results from the procedures and policies of the advertising agency. When this happens, the agency has generally gone beyond its ordinary responsibilities and has taken the lead in making sure that all its people thoroughly understand the advertiser's business, his marketing methods, the competition, how advertising can and cannot be of assistance, what has worked before and what has failed, and much more.

As a fundamental first step the agency may draw up a marketing statement and fact book on the company which are distributed to all involved.

Often it is not an easy task to get the necessary information from the company. Company executives who don't know how difficult it is to make advertising succeed feel that all they need do is give the agency a few facts, the agency will come up with something "catchy," and effective advertising will result. Often the agency must refuse to proceed until it has the necessary facts.

It is not enough, however, for the agency to realize it must have facts before it does any planning or creating. The agency must know the questions to ask. The exact questions will depend on the agency's current knowledge of the advertiser's business, on the purpose of the advertising, and on other variables. In any event it is usually necessary for the agency to know the answers to at least the 20 questions that appear below. It is presumed that the ultimate purpose of the advertising is to increase sales of a specified product. If the purpose is something else, such as to recruit employees, some of the questions will be appropriately different.

20 KEY QUESTIONS FOR AN ADVERTISING AGENCY TO ASK A NEW ADVERTISER

1. What is the advertising expected to accomplish?
2. What is the precise product being sold?
3. How does the company's product differ from competing products and services?
4. What are the normal channels of distribution?
5. If there is more than one, what are the percentage of sales produced through each?
6. What are the current buyers of the product like—their socio-economic group, sex, geographic concentration, attitudes, etc.)?
7. What research, if any, has been conducted regarding customers, non-customers, dealers, attitudes, awareness, and motivation for buying?
8. What are believed to be the factors that influence customers' purchasing decisions?
9. What have sales been in recent years?
10. How do sales compare with competitors' in size?
11. In trend?
12. What are the reasons for the brand's share of market and the trend of sales?

13. What are the marketing goals for the coming year?
14. What are the goals for future years?
15. What changes, if any, in the product itself or in the marketing methods are planned for the coming year and for future years?
16. What were the advertising budgets in past years?
17. Have the results been satisfactory?
18. If not, why not?
19. What is the advertising budget for the coming year? If none has been established, would the company like the agency to make a recommendation?
20. How will the effectiveness of the advertising be measured?

If the advertising agency asks these questions, and follows up on the questions they raise – and if the agency has the necessary competence and experience in marketing, media, copy, and art – and if the agency has an attitude of putting the advertiser's interest before its own – and if the agency is able to tactfully convince the advertiser to follow its sound recommendations – it is possible that the advertising will succeed largely through the agency's efforts.

More often, however, the advertising director, the chief executive officer, or someone else in authority at the company deserves the primary credit for successful advertising. This person usually has some previous experience in advertising, generally in an advertising agency. He has one advantage over people in the agency: He is better able to convince his associates of the soundness of certain advertising decisions. They know him. They trust him. And he knows them – their foibles and their self-interests. More than anything else, however, he has a determination to make the advertising succeed. He knows that the many parts of an ad are like links in a chain. If any one link is weak, the chain won't pull in much money. He knows that while he may make many correct decisions, only one wrong decision will cause the advertising to fail. He therefore allows no decisions to be based on anything except what will make for the most effective advertising.

While he must be knowledgeable about advertising, the experts at the advertising agency necessarily know more than he. His talent is to get the most out of the agency. He doesn't know the answers, but he knows something much more important – the questions to ask, either of the agency or of himself, as he looks at or listens to agency recommendations.

10 KEY QUESTIONS FOR AN ADVERTISER TO ASK ABOUT AN AGENCY'S RECOMMENDATIONS

1. Why is the type of medium (television, radio, newspapers, magazines, car card, outdoor) or combination of types recommended?
2. Why those specific stations, that network, those publications, or those locations?
3. Why that size ad or that length commercial?
4. Why that frequency?
5. Will the beginning of each advertisement or commercial attract and select prospects for what is being sold?
6. Is the copy long enough to arouse the desired feeling or action or emotion?
7. Is the copy too long for the medium or the inherent interest of the product?
8. Is the final effect of each advertisement or commercial directly related to the next step (such as choosing a package or being receptive to a salesman's call) in the marketing?
9. As a whole, will the advertisement or commercial cause large numbers of people to buy the product immediately, soon, or eventually?
10. What parallel successes in media selection and creative approach can the agency point to?

It will take more than solid answers to these questions for the advertising to succeed. The judgments of the agency and the advertiser in each instance must be correct, for example. However, answers to these questions make it possible for the advertiser to make intelligent judgments.

Usually neither the agency nor the advertiser alone is responsible for the success of the advertising. They have a joint responsibility, with each respecting yet checking the other, and with both contributing to the eventual results. In the most successful relationships, each anticipates the other's questions.

Fundamental to the success of any advertising—whether the agency or the advertiser takes the lead, or the leadership is joint—is the selection of the advertising agency. A sound choice can be made by a competent executive with little experience in advertising if he asks questions like these:

7 QUESTIONS FOR AN ADVERTISER TO ASK
WHEN CHOOSING AN ADVERTISING AGENCY

1. Which of your clients market their products or services the way we do?
2. How successful has your advertising been for them?
3. Whom can I call at those clients for more information?
4. Is our account likely to be profitable enough for you to put forth your best efforts?
5. Who will actually work on our account?
6. What is their experience and record of success in advertising products or services marketed the ways ours are?
7. How do you suggest the effectiveness of the advertising be measured?

If the advertiser asks these questions, follows up the answers, and has the judgment to choose an appropriate agency – and if the advertiser and the agency exchange the information indicated by the previous questions in this chapter – and if the 27 most common mistakes in advertising are avoided – the advertising campaign may be one of those that succeeds to the extent promised by the agency and expected by the advertiser.

The monetary rewards from a successful campaign can be sizable – for the company, for executives of the company, and for account, creative, and media people at the advertising agency.

The emotional rewards can be even greater. Successful advertising calls for the same kind of cooperation among skillful specialists that winning at football does. The coach and the quarterback – that is, the advertising director and the account executive – may get most of the glory. But there's plenty of opportunity for running backs and wide receivers – copywriters and art directors – to star. And no one can look good unless everyone on the team does his or her job competently.

It is beauty in action. It is competitive. And it is typically American.

147

GLOSSARY OF COMMONLY USED ADVERTISING TERMS

account executive Salesman, in the highest sense of the word, for an advertising agency. His principal responsibilities are communicating the goals of the advertiser, as well as other appropriate information, to other members of the agency, and in turn explaining to the advertiser why the agency's recommendations will accomplish what the advertiser wishes.

account supervisor The account executive's boss in a large advertising agency.

ADI Area of Dominant Influence, the geographical area reached by a television station. Program ratings are stated in terms of the percentage of homes reached in an Area of Dominant Influence. For example, an ADI of 13 means that the program is tuned into by 13 percent of the homes in the counties served.

advertising agency An accredited advertising agency is a company to which media pay 15 percent of the dollar value of advertising space or time. Advertising agencies not accredited by the media are sales promotion agencies in masquerade.

advertising boutique A firm that specializes in creating advertising, generally TV commercials. Normally used by the advertiser in conjunction with a time-buying agency.

advertising director The man or woman in charge of advertising at the advertising company.

advertising manager The person in the advertising company who is responsible for day-to-day communication with the advertising agency. Often used interchangeably with advertising director, although the latter title is more prestigious.

ANA The biggest trade organization of advertisers, Association of National Advertisers.

brand manager The executive responsible for marketing a product under a specific name, such as Maxwell House.

brand name index Measures the sales of a number of different products and brands.

contract The number of lines, pages, or number of insertions an advertiser promises to buy in a medium during a year. The larger the number of lines, pages, or insertions, the lower the advertising line rate.

copy The words in an advertisement or commercial.

copywriter One who writes advertisements and commercials.

cost per inquiry A calculation used to measure the effectiveness of direct response advertisements. If an advertisement costs $2,000 and 400 people respond, the cost per inquiry is $2,000 divided by 400, or $5. This calculation makes it possible to compare the pulling power of different publications, and of different-size advertisements.

direct mail Actually a redundant phrase because it describes the use of the mail for mass communications *from* the advertiser. However, the use of "direct" serves to eliminate confusion with "mail order," which uses space advertising, and instructs the reader to write to the advertiser.

direct response More inclusive than "mail order." Advertising that aims at eliciting any kind of immediate action (by mail, telephone, or a personal visit) from the reader, viewer, or listener.

discount The amount some publications allow for prompt payment of bills, almost always 2 percent.

four A's The biggest advertising agency trade organization, American Association of Advertising Agencies.

four-color The use of all the primary colors plus black.

full-service agency The usual kind of advertising agency, providing, at the minimum, creative services, media analysis and recommendations, research, and sales promotion. Contrasts with the advertising boutique or the time-buying agency.

layout The rough design of the advertisement.

letterpress The commonest method of printing until the mid-20th century. The type or illustration is raised slightly above the non-printing areas on the plate; the ink adheres to the raised surface, and is transferred to paper.

line A measurement of depth in printing. A newspaper advertisement is usually described as being so many columns wide by so many lines deep. A quarter newspaper page ad, for example, in a typical eight-column newspaper is 4 columns wide by 150 lines deep, or a total of 600 lines. (A full page in a typical 8-column newspaper consists of 2,400 lines.)

line rate The charge made by a newspaper for an advertisement. For example, for a quarter-page advertisement (600 lines) in a newspaper with a rate of $3.00 per line, the space cost is $1,800.

lipsync Jargon for the words in the audio portion of a television commercial, which are in synchronization with the lips of the speaker.

logo Short for "logotype," the name of the advertiser set in a specific self-identifying typestyle.

mail order Advertising that aims at eliciting responses by mail from prospects, either orders for merchandise or inquiries for more information. Not to be confused with direct mail.

management supervisor The account supervisor's boss in a large advertising agency.

marketing Distributing products or services at a profit. Differs from "selling" in that selling is only one of the tools of marketing.

mat A mold made of an advertisement and sent to a publication using the letterpress method of printing.

mechanical An accurate paste-up suitable for reproduction of the type and illustrations of an advertisement or booklet.

media An umbrella term that includes all means of communication that accept advertising: television networks and stations, radio networks and stations, newspapers, magazines, newspaper supplements, outdoor advertising companies, transit advertising companies, or any other. The singular, seldom used, is medium.

media buyer The person at the advertising agency who enters orders to media specifying the sizes of ads, dates of placement, costs, and other conditions.

montage In a print advertisement, an arrangement of illustrations, often used in movie advertising. Also, in a TV commercial, a rapid succession of short takes, often still shots.

Nielsen A method of measuring the number of home sets tuned to a television program. Reports are based on a sample of about 1,000 homes. Ratings are in terms of a percentage of the number of television households. A national rating of 25, for example, means that 25 percent of all television homes were tuned to the program.

offset A method of printing. Actually short for photo-lithography or photo-offset. Instead of relying on raised surfaces for delineation of the image (as in letterpress), offset uses the natural antipathy of water to grease. Ink is deposited on the areas to be printed which have been greased, and the greasy ink is rejected by the water-treated non-printing areas.

pica A measurement of width in printing.

position Most commonly used to describe the location of an advertisement in a publication, as "we got a lousy position." Also may be used in connection with an advertising and/or marketing technique of positioning.

positioning Basing the copy strategy primarily on the relationship between the advertisers' sales and the sales of the leader in the industry.

premium Used in two entirely different ways: (1) The charge for a specified position in a publication or (2) a free or low-cost gift offered in an advertisement.

premium position A desirable page in a magazine or newspaper for which the advertiser pays extra. A prime example is the back cover.

printer A company that produces in quantity booklets, handbooks, sometimes proofs of advertisements, newspapers, magazines, and so on. Differs from a typographer.

producer The person at the agency who selects or recommends the television production company and who communicates with it. While he must in many ways fulfill the same responsibilities as the producer of a feature motion picture film, he has much less power.

product manager The executive responsible for marketing a specific commodity or manufactured item. In an aluminum company, for example, there might be a product manager for sheet, another for ingot, a third for wire, etc.

production company The company that photographs the television commercial or motion picture film and supplies accompanying expertise.

production cost The cost of setting an advertisement in type, taking photographs or having illustrations made, making plates, shipping advertising material to the medium, etc. That is, the cost of preparing an advertisement or commercial for publication.

proof A reproduction of an advertisement pulled by a typographer from type.

publicity Mention of a company in a medium otherwise than by means of an advertisement or commercial.

public relations agency A company that specializes in helping corporations with their communications to various sections of the public.

rate card Issued by each medium showing rates, closing dates, mechanical requirements, and so on.

reproduction proof A high-quality proof of the advertisement used to make printing plates or sent directly to publications that use the offset method of printing.

reverse Printing white on black.

rough cut An unfinished version of a television commercial or motion picture.

sanserif A typeface without serifs. Examples: Futura, Folio.

script A written version of a radio or television commercial.

serif In a typeface, the fine lines that project from the main strokes of the letters. Examples of serif typefaces: Garamond, Goudy.

Simmons A method of measuring the readership of publications, which is the sum of the circulation plus pass-along readership.

space The actual area an ad in a print medium occupies.

space cost How much an advertiser pays to the medium through the advertising agency.

space salesman One who represents a print medium.

speculative presentation The advertisements and/or commercials plus media recommendations and other ideas shown to an advertiser by a prospective advertising agency.

Standard Rate & Data A publication that contains data about media— rates, closing dates, mechanical requirements, and so on.

Starch score The most common method of measuring the attention gained by and the readership of a printed advertisement. From the name of the founder of the company, Daniel Starch.

story board A series of drawings or still photographs showing the video portion of a television commercial with the audio portion and other information typed underneath.

time What television and radio stations and networks sell; the equivalent for a commercial of the space occupied by a print ad.

time buyer A member of an agency who enters orders to networks and stations specifying the program or spot to be used, the price and conditions.

time-buying agency An advertising agency that specializes in negotiating availability and rates, generally TV time. Contrasted with a full-service agency.

traffic manager The person at the agency who makes sure that advertising materials such as reproduction proofs, mats, film, and tapes get where they should on time, both inside the agency and out.

two-color The use of black ink plus one other color of ink, usually on white paper. However, paper may be any color, and any two colors of ink may be used.

typeface The style of the type, such as Garamond, Bodoni, Cooper, Futura, Goudy.

typographer One who sets the type for an advertisement, submits proofs for OK or correction, then pulls reproduction proofs, or "repros."

voice over Used to describe the audio portion of a television commercial when the speaker is not on camera. As opposed to lipsync.

INDEX

advertiser
  agency's recommendations
    and, 146
  choosing an agency, 147
  critical decisions of, 143
agencies, advertising
  Batten, Barton, Durstine &
    Osborn, 100
  Benn & MacDonough, 16, 73
  Conahay & Lyon, 120
  Doyle Dane Bernbach, 52
  Gumpertz, Bentley, Fried,
    Scott, 99
  J. Walter Thompson, 50, 70
  Kallir, Philips, Ross, 38
  Ketchum, MacLeod, & Grove,
    76
  Mintz & Hoke, 100
  Marsteller, 16
  Ogilvy & Mather, 135
  S. R. Leon, 97
  Young & Rubicam, 120
agency, advertising
  advantages of using, 20
  marketing experience of, 19
  prefers TV advertising, 22
  questions to ask advertisers,
    144–145
Alexander's, 52–54

American Association of
    Advertising Agencies, 7
art directors
  antagonism toward words, 46–
    47
  corporate logo and, 47–48
artwork, use of, 43–44
audience narcissism and
    advertising copy, 55–57
Avis, 89

backfiring advertising, 87
Batten, Barton, Durstine &
    Osborn, 100
Benn & MacDonough, 16, 73
Bodine, 56, 65–68
Bowery Savings Bank, The, 136–
    137
brand vs. product advantage, 99–
    100
  two common mistakes in, 23
Burke Marketing Research,
    120

C & P Telephone, 73–74
campaigns, advertising
  Alexander's, 52–54
  Avis, 89
  Bodine, 56, 65–68

campaigns, advertising
(*continued*)
  Bowery Savings Bank, The,
    136–137
  C & P Telephone, 73–74
  Diaparene Baby Washcloths,
    99–100
  Elmer's Glue, 120–123
  Federal Express, 24
  Gaines-Burgers, 117–120
  Hanes Corporation, 91–95
  Honeywell, 89
  ITT, 24, 61
  Lanier Dictating Equipment,
    15–16
  L'eggs, 57, 91–95
  Loctite Company, 100–102
  Manufacturers Bank (Cal.), 97–
    99
  Mitchum's Antiperspirants,
    96–97
  Moody's, 16–17, 56, 79
  Parker Pen, 48–50, 56
  Schaefer Beer, 88
  Seven-Up, 89
  Tylenol, 36–38
  U. S. Marine Corps, 70
  Virginia Slims, 68–70
  Volkswagen, 51–52, 89, 90–91
car cards, 135–137
categorizing advertising,
  methods of, 41–42
commercials, radio
  Lanier Dictating Equipment,
    15–16
  Manufacturers Bank, (Cal.),
    97–99
commercials, TV
  The Bowery Savings Bank,
    136–137
  C & P Telephone, 73–74
  dealer-oriented, 24
  Federal Express, 24–27
  ITT, 24
  Schaefer Beer, 88
Conahay & Lyon, 120
copy testing
  see measuring effectiveness of
    advertising

copywriting, principles of, 77–78
  audience attitude and, 80–82,
    95
  competition and, 86–89, 91
  nature of audience and, 84–85
  nature of medium and, 82–84
  nature of product and, 85–86, 91
  purpose of advertising and, 78–
    80
cost of advertising, 128–131
  choice of agency and, 18–19
  costs breakdown, 130
  creative fees, 131
  usual rate of compensation, 128
creativity
  in content, 48–54
  excessive expectations of, 39
  in form, 43–48
  size of advertisement and, 39
criticisms of advertising, 132–137

Diaparene Baby Washcloths, 99–
  100
differentiating advertising goals,
  40–42
DiMaggio, Joe, 137
direct mail, 124–127
  administrator of, 125
  common mistakes in, 126–127
  copywriters, 125
  enclosures, 126
  facilitating response, 126–127,
    137
  Friday mailings, 126
  high cost of, 124
  impersonal copy, 126
  mailing lists and records, 125
  response to, 124
  see also direct response
    advertising
direct response advertising, 13–
  14, 30–31, 32–33, 41, 65, 79, 81,
  86–87, 103, 105
  see also direct mail
Doyle Dane Bernbach, 52

effectiveness of advertising, 5–7
  choice of agency and, 11–14
  exaggerated claims for, 133

mass production and, 132–133
see also mistakes in
advertising, size of
advertisement
Elmer's Glue, 120–123
executive, advertising, 2–4
executive, corporate, and
responsibility for
advertising, 9–10, 45, 90

fact book, corporation, 143
factual advertising, 52–54
Federal Express, 24–27
frequency of advertising, 30–31
character of product and, 33
creativity and, 39
on radio and TV, 32, 33
salesmen's calls and, 41
size of advertisement and, 32–33
funeral service advertising, 86

Gaines-Burgers, 117–120
General Mills, 1
GPC Corporation, 1
Gumpertz, Bentley, Fried, Scott, 99

Hanes Corporation, 91–95
Henry V (Shakespeare), 60–61, 62
Honeywell Corporation, 89

identification advertising
corporate, 79, 80
image, 59–63, 68–73
negative, 70, 72, 73
positive and negative, 64–65
promise advertising and, 65, 73–74
illustrations
drawings and photographs, 43–44
multiple, 44
imitative advertising, 40–42
intangible services, advertising of, 86
ITT, 24, 61

J. Walter Thompson, 50

Kallir, Philips, Ross, 38
Ketchum, MacLeod, & Grove, 74

Lanier Dictating Equipment, 15–16
L'eggs, 57, 91–95
Loctite Company, 100–102
logo, corporate, 47
low-rate advertising, 28–29

Manufacturers Bank (Cal.), 97–99
marketing statement, 143
market researchers, 112
Marsteller agency, 16
measuring effectiveness of
advertising, 103–123
attitude studies, 113
awareness studies, 111–112
before-and-after studies, 111–113
focus group interview, 109–110
matched samples technique, 107–108
ostensible program testing, 108
recall of sales points, 107
regional addition, 110–111
six-city testing, 108
split runs, 110, 113
see mistakes in advertising,
size of advertisement
Mintz & Hoke Inc., 100
mistakes in advertising
advertiser doing agency's
work, 23, 139
advertiser handling direct mail
himself, 124–127, 142
applying sound copy principle
at wrong time, 78–79, 141
choosing medium for low rate,
28–29, 139
choosing wrong advertising
agency, 11–14, 138
creating for presentations, not
for the medium, 45, 140
differing in form, not in
content, 45, 140
expecting too much from
creativity, 39, 139

mistakes in advertising
(continued)
entertaining instead of selling,
57–58, 140
failing to arouse the right
emotions, 62–63, 141
failing to capitalize on product,
86, 141
failing to utilize advantages of
medium, 84–86, 141
having no measure of
effectiveness, 113, 142
imitating, 40–42, 139
making advertisement too big,
34–38, 139
making fun of prospect, 56–57,
140
making logo wrong size, 47–48,
140
not advertising frequently
enough, 30–31, 139
not concentrating
advertisement on viewer, 55–
56, 140
not realizing limitations of
Starch scores, 104–107, 141
over-creativity with type, 46–
47, 140
overestimating effect of
advertising, 132–133, 142
pleasing advertiser's chief
executive officer, 103–104, 141
promoting sale of competitor's
brand, 87–89, 141
putting wrong company official
in charge, 9–10, 138
too much or too litte, 21–23, 138
using a pun in a headline, 57,
140
Mitchum's Antiperspirants, 96–
97
Moody's 16–17, 56, 79

Ogilvy & Mather, 135

package good advertising, 11–12,
30–31, 41, 79, 81, 82, 87, 106
Parker Pen, 48–50, 56

photography, use of, 44, 45–46
positioning, 87–89, 96–102
Proctor & Gamble, 1
promise advertising
combined with identification
advertising, 65, 73–74
positive and negative
advertising, 64

radio–television advertising, and
print advertising, 82–84
retail advertising, brand name,
13, 41
Richard III (Shakespeare), 59–60,
62

Schaefer Beer, 88
Seven-Up, 89
size of advertisement
creativity and, 39
frequency of appearance and,
32, 33, 34–35
mistake of bigness and, 34, 36
nature of medium and, 36
Tylenol's success with small
advertisements, 38
small-budget advertisers, 129–
131
speculative presentations, 11, 19
S. R. Leon Agency, 97
Starch, Daniel, 104, 115
Starch scores, 104–107, 113

tastefulness and vulgarity, uses
of, 85
Tylenol, 36–38

U. S. Marine Corp., 70

Virginia Slims, 68–70
Volkswagen, 50–52, 89, 90–91
vulgarity in advertising
see tastefulness and vulgarity

women's movement and Virginia
Slims, 68

Young & Rubicam, 120

AMACOM Executive Books-Paperbacks

John D. Arnold	The Art of Decision Making: 7 Steps to Achieving More Effective Results	$6.95
Eugene L. Benge	Elements of Modern Management	$5.95
Alec Benn	The 27 Most Common Mistakes in Advertising	$5.95
Dudley Bennett	TA and the Manager	$6.95
Warren Bennis	The Unconscious Conspiracy	$5.95
Don Berliner	Want a Job? Get Some Experience...	$5.95
Borst & Montana	Managing Nonprofit Organizations	$6.95
J. Douglas Brown	The Human Nature of Organizations	$5.95
Ronald D. Brown	From Selling to Managing	$5.95
Richard E. Byrd	A Guide to Personal Risk Taking	$5.95
Logan Cheek	Zero-Base Budgeting Comes of Age	$6.95
William A. Cohen	The Executive's Guide to Finding a Superior Job	$5.95
Richard R. Conarroe	Bravely, Bravely in Business	$4.95
Ken Cooper	Bodybusiness	$5.95
James J. Cribbin	Effective Managerial Leadership	$6.95
John D. Drake	Interviewing for Managers	$5.95
Richard J. Dunsing	You and I Have Simply Got to Stop Meeting This Way	$5.95
Sidney Edlund	There Is a Better Way to Sell	$5.95
Elam & Paley	Marketing for the Nonmarketing Executive	$5.95
Norman L. Enger	Management Standards for Developing Information Systems	$6.95
Figueroa & Winkler	A Business Information Guidebook	$9.95
Saul W. Gellerman	Motivation and Productivity	$6.95
Roger A. Golde	Muddling Through	$5.95
Bernard Haldane	Career Satisfaction and Success	$5.95
Lois B. Hart	Moving Up! Women and Leadership	$6.95
Hart & Schleicher	A Conference and Workshop Planner's Manual	$15.95
Michael Hayes	Pay Yourself First: The High Beta/No-Load Way to Stock Market Profits	$6.95
Maurice R. Hecht	What Happens in Management	$7.95
Charles L. Hughes	Goal Setting	$5.95
John W. Humble	How to Manage By Objectives	$5.95
Jones & Trentin	Budgeting (rev. ed.)	$12.95
Donald P. Kenney	Minicomputers	$7.95
Ray A. Killian	Managing Human Resources	$6.95
William H. Krause	How to Hire and Motivate Manufacturers' Representatives	$6.95

Sy Lazarus	A Guide to Effective Communication	$5.95
Wayne A. Lemmon	The Owner's and Manager's Market Analysis Workbook for Small to Moderate Retail and Service Establishments	$9.95
Philip R. Lund	Compelling Selling	$5.95
Dale D. McConkey	No-Nonsense Delegation	$5.95
Michael E. McGill	Organization Development for Operating Managers	$6.95
Robert J. McKain, Jr.	Realize Your Potential	$5.95
Edward S. McKay	The Marketing Mystique	$6.95
Milam & Crumbley	Estate Planning	$6.95
Donald E. Miller	The Meaningful Interpretation of Financial Statements	$6.95
Robert L. Montgomery	Memory Made Easy	$5.95
Terry A. Mort	Systematic Selling: How to Influence the Buying Decision Process	$6.95
Oxenfeldt, Miller & Dickinson	A Basic Approach to Executive Decision Making	$7.95
Dean B. Peskin	A Job Loss Survival Manual	$5.95
Andrew Pleninger	How To Survive and Market Yourself in Management	$6.95
Elton T. Reeves	So You Want to Be a Supervisor (rev. ed.)	$6.95
Paula I. Robbins	Successful Midlife Career Change	$7.95
Edward Roseman	Confronting Nonpromotability	$5.95
William E. Rothschild	Putting It All Together	$7.95
H. Lee Rust	Jobsearch	$7.95
Hank Seiden	Advertising Pure and Simple	$5.95
Robert Seidenberg	Corporate Wives... Corporate Casualties?	$6.95
Roger W. Seng	The Skills of Selling	$7.95
Andrew H. Souerwine	Career Strategies	$7.95
Summer & Levy, eds.	Microcomputers for Business	$7.95
Erwin S. Stanton	Successful Personnel Recruiting and Selection	$8.95
Curtis W. Symonds	Basic Financial Management (rev. ed.)	$5.95
William C. Waddell	Overcoming Murphy's Law	$5.95
Murray L. Weidenbaum	The Future of Business Regulation	$5.95
Allen Weiss	Write What You Mean	$5.95
Leon A. Wortman	Successful Small Business Management	$5.95
Wortman & Sperling	Defining the Manager's Job (rev. ed.)	$9.95
Jere E. Yates	Managing Stress	$5.95